$martEssentials™

for

SELLING YOUR HOME

$martEssentials™

for

SELLING YOUR HOME

How To Get The Highest Price In The Shortest Time

Deborah Rhoney

Dan Gooder Richard
SMART ESSENTIALS Series Editor

Inkspiration Media

SMART ESSENTIALS™ FOR SELLING YOUR HOME:
How To Get The Highest Price In The Shortest Time

Published by:
Inkspiration Media
2724 Dorr Avenue, Suite 103, Fairfax, VA 22031
http://www.SmartEssentials.com

ISTC: A0320120000B4760
Library of Congress Control Number: 2012921778

Publisher's Cataloging-In-Publication Data
(Prepared by The Donohue Group, Inc.)

Rhoney, Deborah, 1953 –
    Smart Essentials™ for selling your home : how to get the highest price
in the shortest time / Deborah Rhoney.
        p. ; cm. — (Smart Essentials™ series)
    ISBN-13: 978-1-939319-01-2
    ISBN-10: 1-939319-01-3
    1. House selling — United States. 2. Residential real estate —
United States. I. Title. II. Title: Selling your home
HD259 .R46 2013
643/.12/0973   2012921778

CONTENTS

CHAPTER 1
ROADMAP

How to sell your home for the highest price in the shortest time.
Selling your home in your local market — even in today's toughest
markets — means staying focused on the essentials . . . and not being
distracted by the collateral chatter that surrounds the large, nail-biting,
life-shaping sale of one of your largest assets.

To market your home effectively, you first need a roadmap of all the
elements involved. Then you can concentrate on the pieces that you
control . . . and leave the details to the professionals.

With that in mind, here are the 10 essential steps to selling your home.

10 KEY STEPS TO SELLING YOUR HOME

1. **Pick a real estate agent** who will help you choose the best asking
   price and marketing plan to get your home sold. (In today's market,
   you'll find selling without professional representation difficult,
   at best.)

2. **Review all your marketing options,** including financing,
   incentives and other deal "sweeteners" to beat the competition to a
   fast sale.

3. **Make repairs or improvements** that will increase the
   marketability of your home.

4. **List your home** for sale at a smart price.

5. **Make it easy for your home** to be shown to prospective buyers.

6. **Consider offers** and negotiate the best sales contract on
   your terms.

7. **Order inspections,** if they're your responsibility as seller.

8. **Stand by as appraisals,** surveys and inspections are conducted and
   your buyer lines up financing.

9. **Go to settlement.**[††]

10. **Move out** of your old home and into your new life.

> ††**Settlement**
> The process of finalizing the sales contract between buyer and seller. In some areas, this is referred to as "closing" or "escrow." Throughout this guide, we'll simply call it settlement, which may take place in an office, where both parties (and usually their representatives) come together to sign final documents and exchange funds. In other cases, settlement may be handled from separate locations.

Still, not everything will go perfectly. Now that you've seen the roadmap ahead, this is where things can get hairy. Let's get down to the nitty-gritty — the top 10 costliest mistakes even smart sellers make.

TOP 10 REALLY BIG SELLING MISTAKES TO AVOID

Once you've made a big selling mistake, it is often too late to correct it. That's why we're sharing the 10 worst mistakes most home sellers make right up front. Avoid them and you'll be well on your way to a successful sale.

1. **Setting the wrong price.** Picking the right listing price sells a home faster than any other factor. Underpricing a home could cost you money — lots of it! Overpricing a home can yield the exact same result — except it will take longer to get there. We'll explain more later.

2. **Selling "as-is" condition.** In today's competitive market, most buyers won't even consider a home that needs repairs. They're looking for attractive, move-in condition — think model home. Buyers who must tackle fix-ups will lower their offers accordingly. You'll pay the costs one way or another, so you might as well get those issues handled beforehand and speed the sale of your home.

3. **Ignoring curb appeal.** What your home looks like on the outside — its "curb appeal" — is one of the most essential factors to a successful sale (right up there with pricing). Online home shoppers tend to fall in love with a home they see on the Internet. But a positive impression online can be undone at the curb by unkempt landscaping, peeling paint, crooked shutters, etc. Those deal-killing mistakes will not be counteracted by the most-perfect floor plan or a tasteful interior — assuming the buyer even bothers to go inside.

4. **Overlooking cosmetics.** Dirt just doesn't sell — clean everything! It's fast, it's cheap and it pays off handsomely, even if you have to hire a service. The next best dollar-for-dollar investment for selling your home: fresh paint in neutral colors. After that, consider new carpeting — replaced for either condition or color. You'll learn plenty about this topic later in the guide.

5. **Lavishly over-improving.** While it's important to fix, clean and brighten your home to get it ready for sale, steer clear of major/expensive improvements that won't return their cost at sale time. Spending too much on remodeling projects just drains money from your net proceeds. (However, some major projects, like replacing a roof, should be done if they're needed.)

6. **Being inflexible about financing.** The more buyers you can appeal to in terms of financing, the greater your chances of selling faster. Be flexible about accepting Federal Housing Administration (FHA) and Veterans Affairs (VA) financing, offering seller financing, paying settlement costs, providing a decorating allowance or other incentives attractive to buyers.

7. **Falling prey to "General Custer syndrome."** Resist the urge to go it alone. Hiring a professional real estate agent is likely to be your fastest way to a home sale at a great price. Be sure to tap all the expertise you can — online sites, a stager, photographer, real estate attorney, professional inspectors, etc.

8. **Being underfoot.** Don't be at home when your home is being shown. Take the kids and pets elsewhere, if possible. If you are working with an agent, allow that person to show your home alone. Buyers are more comfortable looking at homes when the homeowners are not around.

9. **Putting up your dukes.** No one wins if you enter negotiations wearing mental boxing gloves. Approach negotiations in a positive frame of mind. After all, you and the buyer both want the same thing — a sale. Remain flexible.

10. **Letting a buyer's offer languish.** Essential final thought: One of the most important moves you can make is to reply immediately to an offer — even if it's not the offer you were looking for. When buyers make an offer they are, right then, in the mood to buy, but moods can change quickly. If you can't accept the offer outright, make your counteroffer quickly. You never know what buyers will accept until you ask!

CHAPTER 1

ROADMAP

We Respect Your Time And Won't Waste It On Meaningless Filler

We know you're smart. (Buying **SMART ESSENTIALS FOR SELLING YOUR HOME** proves it . . . at least to us.) And we know your time is precious. You don't need to spend it slogging through endless pages of information that's irrelevant to getting your home sold.

Side trips like deciding to sell, green home improvements (rather than cosmetic fix-ups), sample contracts and inspector reports, settlement documents explained line by line, renting rather than selling, estate sales, flipping houses and moving tips are not here. Why? Because you can leave these details to the professionals . . . or those subjects are better treated separately in unique SMART ESSENTIALS guides specifically for those niche readers.

You don't need to be a real estate expert. What you need is to sell your home for the best price in the shortest time. Yet you are smart enough to know you'll need to work with several professionals during this complex — and sometimes stressful — milestone transaction. We'll tell you how you can use the expertise of professionals to pull off a sale at the right price and within your timetable.

What You'll Take Away From This Guide

What you *will* find in this SMART ESSENTIALS guide are concise, practical, insider strategies to do three things:

- ▶ Get the highest possible price for your home.
- ▶ Save time and sell on your timetable.
- ▶ Avoid the costliest mistakes even smart home sellers make.

How This SMART ESSENTIALS Guide Is Organized

There are seven essential strategies you must get right from the start, which shape the sections to this SMART ESSENTIALS guide:

ROADMAP: Follow the essential roadmap and avoid the costliest selling mistakes.

TEAM: Find the right real estate agent and build your selling team.

MONEY: Determine your home's market value, compute net proceeds, understand tax implications.

● **PRICE:** Price your home to sell for top dollar in your market.

● **PREPARE:** Spend only what is necessary to prepare your home to sell fast.

● **SHOW:** Present your home to make buyers fall in love at first sight.

● **NEGOTIATE:** Counteroffer to get the best contract that fits your timetable.

We Want To Hear From You. Early And Often!

Nothing informs our readers as much as stories from other Smarties . . . what they did right, stupid mistakes they can laugh about (now), and advice on tricky choices they had to make along the road of good intentions. Come back regularly to our website at *http://www.SmartEssentials.com*. Share your experience. Lurk over the amazing tips and slips other Smarties experienced. Join the community. Tell us how we can do better in the next edition. (We're smart, but we're not perfect. Yet.) We love your stories! And we know other Smarties do, too.

Now let's cut to the chase. First stop: Find and hire a top-notch real estate professional.

Chapter 1 Roundup

Smart Essentials ROADMAP :: What You Have Learned

▶▶ 10 key steps to selling your home.
▶▶ Top 10 really big selling mistakes to avoid.
▶▶ Why we respect your time and skip the filler.
▶▶ What you'll take away from this guide.
▶▶ How this SMART ESSENTIALS guide is organized.
▶▶ We want to hear from you.

Smart Essentials

Page	Essential Note

CHAPTER 2

TEAM

In this chapter, you'll learn smart ways to:

1. Know what an agent can do for you.

2. Select a top-notch real estate agent to sell your home.

3. Decide if your situation fits being a For Sale By Owner.

HIRING A REAL ESTATE PROFESSIONAL

The major reason homeowners consider selling "by owner" is to save the cost of commissions/fees for professional representation—which can be thousands of dollars. Depending on your contract, you might pay a percentage of the final sale price (the most typical arrangement), or a flat fee, hourly rate or fee-per-service basis. Rates vary and are officially negotiable. (Getting a break is the secret.)

Agents Versus Brokers

When you sign a contract for real estate representation, known as a "listing agreement," you're actually signing a contract with two parties—an agent and a broker (although your agent could also *be* the broker). Think of the "agent" as the salesperson for the broker, who operates the "brokerage company." The listing agent is the individual who works with you personally to market your home.

By law, only a broker, who has passed a special exam, can receive a brokerage commission. When an agent/salesperson represents a broker in a transaction—rather than the broker working personally with the seller—the broker splits the brokerage commission with the salesperson.

Your listing agent and broker may not receive all of the commission/fees from the sale of your home, however. Actually, the commission is frequently split as many as four ways—among your listing agent and broker (the "listing side") and among the agent and broker who bring the buyer to the contract (the "buying side").

TEAM

The agent who produces the buyer may be a "seller's agent" (working for the seller) or a "buyer's agent" (working for the buyer). In most listing agreements, sellers offer a commission or fees not only to their own listing agent and broker, but also to agents/brokers who produce a buyer for the home. Here's where it gets hairy: Those "co-brokers" are actually working for the seller, too—*unless* the buyer has hired a buyer's agent through a buyer's representation contract.

A buyer's agent is one who is under contract to represent the interests of the buyer. The fee or commission for a buyer's agent may be paid by the seller, the buyer, or negotiated between buyer and seller. In most cases, the seller's commission/fees are shared with the cooperating buyer's agent and broker. Regardless of whether the buyer is found by a listing salesperson or a buyer's agent, anyone with a real estate license is required to treat both the seller and the buyer honestly.

◆ ◆ ◆

Essential Takeaway

Essential Takeaway: Think about this: The seller's commission/fee typically pays for the buyer's agent services. That means if you are selling by-owner instead, to avoid paying a commission, then (1) agents working with buyers have no incentive to show your home for sale, and (2) their buyers may be shocked to discover they must pay their agent's commission/fees if they purchase your by-owner home . . . when most of the other competing home sellers will pay those commission/fees. In a nutshell, many by-owner sellers end up saving only half the full commission/fees because they often end up paying the buyer's agent and broker or they lower the price of their home to compensate for the buyer having to do so.

◆ ◆ ◆

| **What Your Realty Commission Buys** | Although you may work personally with either a broker or a salesperson, we use the term "agent" interchangeably throughout this guide for simplicity. |

The reason 90% of sellers use an agent, rather than go the for-sale-by-owner (FSBO; pronounced "Fisbo") route, is that a full-service real estate agent provides services that most sellers simply can't do by themselves:

● **Craft a marketing strategy** targeted to your home and advise you on how best to prepare your home for sale.

● **Provide up-to-date and crucial local market information,** including recent sales, current listings and various statistics, that you may have a hard time finding yourself.

● **Place your property in the Multiple Listing Service (MLS)**[††], which exposes your home to all the buyers working with cooperating member brokers. This effectively puts every agent in town and beyond to work helping to sell your home.

> [††]*Multiple Listing Service (MLS)*
> A network that contains a database of all area homes on the market listed by members of the local MLS. All area members of the MLS have access to the regularly updated information.

● **Advertise your home through various media** — syndicated to online portals and classifieds sites, newspapers, home-guide magazines, emails, websites, social media, direct mail, signage, broker open houses, etc.

● **Conduct open houses and home showings** whether you're at home or not, saving you hours of "minding the store."

● **Provide pre-qualified buyers** who know what they want and how much they can afford. Pre-screening prospects minimizes "sightseers" who have no intention of buying your home and protects you from the threat of "unwelcome" visitors.

● **Show your home to its best advantage.** Buyers often shy away from asking homeowners questions, and homeowners are sometimes defensive about defects or are not forthcoming enough with essential details buyers want — or are too forthcoming with comments that become a disadvantage during negotiations. An agent can answer questions objectively and guide the buyer to a purchase.

● **Help you negotiate a satisfactory sale.** As an experienced mediator, an agent acts as a buffer between the parties to a home sale, helping prevent negotiations from bogging down. Loads more on negotiating in Chapter 7 NEGOTIATE.

● **Lead both you and the buyer through the mortgage maze** of interest rates, points, fees and financing options, and follow up to ensure the buyer's mortgage process is on track.

● **Protect your interests from contract to settlement** with an understanding of local procedures and legal requirements. An experienced agent will smooth the way toward agreements and attend to all the details that must come together before settlement.

● **Provide after-sale advice** and invaluable referrals for all the details from repairs to packing, and from hiring movers to relocating pets.

Strategies To Find The Right Agent

Frankly, not all real estate agents are created equal. Some real estate agents are simply better than others. Smart sellers know the tell-tale signs of a top agent. Here's how:

● **Ask for referrals.** Your friends, relatives and coworkers have probably gone down this trail before and may be able to recommend someone who helped them.

● **Look around your neighborhood.** Whose names show up on the "for sale" signs — more important, the "sold" signs — in your area? Watch your mailbox to see which agents specialize in your neighborhood and are working to get more business. These agents obviously work in and know the community.

● **Shop at open houses.** This can be a great way to see an agent in action — if the open-house agent is the listing agent — while you check out your home's competition. Did the agent ask for your name? Did the agent offer you information on the home and about financing? Did the agent follow up?

● **Consider your chemistry.** Does the agent listen to your questions and concerns, and answer them to your satisfaction? Does the agent respond to your phone calls and emails quickly? You'll want to feel comfortable working with your agent as a consultant who's going to help you sell your largest investment.

● **Ask about the agent's listing activity.** Almost nine out of 10 buyers find the home they purchase through a real estate agent or through agents' marketing from online ads to yard signs. The other 12% of homes are found through word of mouth from friends, neighbors, relatives, builders or knowing the seller. Simply put, agents and their listings generate buyers. Ask how many homes an agent has sold (not just listed) in the last six months, last year and the year before. Increasing numbers means the agent is improving, and so are the agent's systems. Ask for listing-by-listing statistics for (1) days on market (DOM), and (2) list-to-sold prices. Top agents outperform the market and sell their listings for more money and faster than average.

● **Ask for a marketing plan.** Sellers who hire an agent without knowing what they are getting for their money risk not getting their money's worth. What will the agent do for you? Here are some marketing techniques to ask about:

▶ **MLS:** Beyond listing the property, does the agent do listing syndication (pushing listing details with automated services to numerous real estate portal sites online)? Is there an agent website with a My Listings page?

▶ **Online:** Will the agent create a single-property website for your listing? (This is essential.) Virtual tour (still photos or video)? Portal advertising — Realtor.com, Trulia, Zillow, local newspaper, etc.? Classified websites — Craigslist, Backpage, etc.?

▶ **Offline:** Will the agent use direct mail, e.g., just-listed postcards? Homes magazines, newspaper ads? Property flyers?

▶ **Marketability:** What services are offered related to staging, photography, curb appeal, warranty, pre-listing inspections, appraisal? Will the agent arrange self-storage for your extra stuff?

▶ **Yard marketing:** Does the agent provide a yard sign, brochure box, directional signs?

CHAPTER 2

TEAM

▶ **Opens:** Will the agent conduct public open houses for buyers and neighbors? Broker opens for local agents working with buyers? By-appointment-only showings (must contact agent to be prequalified)? How does the agent promote open houses to generate traffic?

▶ **Social media:** Exposure of listing on Facebook and other social media? Video on YouTube?

▶ **Mobile:** Smartphone-compatible listing info on sign, flyers? Quick Response (QR) code links to property website, listing page, virtual tour, video?

▶ **Innovations:** What unique techniques will the agent use to sell your home?

The bottom line: Hire a top-notch pro who has extensive training, strong marketing skills, familiarity with your neighborhood and a solid track record of sales.

Costly Mistakes To Avoid When Selecting A Listing Agent

Not doing in-depth "hire-work" is the single biggest mistake most sellers make (just ahead of asking the wrong price). Here are some doozies:

Mistake #1: Meeting only one or two listing agents before hiring. Most sellers think all agents are the same. Making that assumption could mean your home goes unsold or sells at a lower price.

Solution: Interview several agents, ideally four or more. One smart approach is to ask agents to send you a pre-listing package before your meeting including pricing comparables, market data, home prep tips, agent and brokerage background, services, commission, listing contract, etc. If their "pre-list pack" is professional, then they will also market your property professionally. Invite the best agents — one at a time — to your home for a listing presentation. *Smart Tip:* Some agents like to sign listing contracts in "one trip." Resist any pressure. Sleep on it. Bring back the best on your short list for a second session.

Mistake #2: Hiring an agent because he or she comes in with the highest price recommendation. Inexperienced and promise-the-moon agents tend to "buy listings" by inflating seller expectations with a high listing price. But those listings spend more days on market and often languish until they sell below market value after a death spiral of price reductions.

Solution: Top agents sell for close to list price because they know how to price right in your local market and sell with few or no price reductions. Ask the agent to show you what comparable homes have recently sold for and to prove why the suggested listing price is correct. Be aware that low-ball listers can sell fast, too, but not at the highest possible price.

Mistake #3: Not asking about credentials and not understanding designations. The length of time an agent has been in the business can be misleading. The agent may have been part-time or is a dabbler. Or the agent may have mainly worked with buyers, not sellers.

Solution: Prepare your list of questions before meeting with agents. If the answers you hear don't make sense, or seem vague or incomplete, ask more questions until you're satisfied. Remember: It's the *job* of agents to explain their qualifications, what they intend to do and how they intend to do it.

Mistake #4: Not knowing your preference for a sole practitioner or a team. Some real estate agents work alone, or with a spouse or child, or with one assistant. The best are highly efficient generalists. Others run an outfit with assistants handling details and perhaps several agents, often buyer specialists. Contracting with one business model when you truly prefer the other can be stressful, not to mention costly.

Solution: Solo top agents can be very effective, if they aren't distracted by too many mundane details or too many clients. You could be in great hands, especially if the agent concentrates his or her time on a specialty such as listings only (referring out most buyers), or one large condo complex or development or property type (think golf homes, horse estates, ski chalets or waterfront villas). In short, you get solo attention from one of the best in the area. That said, successful teams are like small companies within a brokerage company. A team's "rainmaker" is often a "closer" for listing presentations and for purchase negotiations. Everything else, from MLS entry to yard signs, from marketing to listing management, and from transaction processing to closing gifts, are handled by staff. With a team, clients may get even more attention faster but from different people, and fewer details are likely to fall through the cracks. *Smart Tip:* Ask agents to detail who does what in their operation and how many transactions a month they manage. Select the business model that matches your comfort level.

DIG DEEPER INTO THE LISTING CONTRACT

Beyond locating a top agent with experience and an active practice, and before hiring a top agent with whom you feel chemistry and comfort sharing personal and financial life details, understand that the devil is in the details of the listing agreement.

**10 Smart Questions
To Ask Before
You Sign**

If not answered in agents' listing packages or presentations, be sure to drill into these details:

1. Can you give me references from your recent sellers?

2. What fee(s) will you charge, and how are they calculated?

3. If I buy my next home through you or through a referral from you, will you discount your listing commission?

4. Do you guarantee your performance, and can I cancel the listing at any time? What is your broker's policy on cancelations?

5. What marketing budget will you invest in my listing? First month? Second 30 days? Following 30 days?

6. How are showing appointments handled? Through you? Me? Lockbox?

7. How often will I hear from you, and what type of feedback should I expect?

8. Will you personally handle contract negotiations, not just pass along buyers' offers to me?

9. Why should I list with you (over the competition)?

10. Do you have any questions for me?

HOW TO KNOW WHEN TO GO FSBO

Selling a home by-owner — without being represented by a real estate professional — can be fraught with difficulties and disappointments. That's not to say it can't be done! If your situation involves one or more of the following factors, selling by-owner might save you a bundle of money in brokerage commissions:

TEAM

● You already have a qualified buyer lined up, or you know several people who have expressed interest in purchasing your home.

● You have a hot property located in a seller's market (rather than a buyer's market),[††] or it's in a very popular neighborhood where the inventory of homes for sale is low compared with high demand from buyers.

● You have significant experience successfully selling previous homes, either by-owner or with representation.

● You are (or have) a real estate attorney who knows the ins and outs of sales contracts and negotiations.

● You are in no hurry to sell and can afford to wait for the right buyer to find you with the offer you want.

> [††] *Seller's Market, Buyer's Market*
>
> A seller's market favors sellers because the inventory of homes is small relative to the number of would-be buyers. It's a buyer's market when there's a large inventory of homes for sale compared with active home shoppers.
>
> So how can you tell what type of market you're in? Ask any agent. Or run the numbers yourself. Look at the Months Supply of Homes metric. In a nutshell, at the current pace of sales, how many months would it take to sell all the homes currently listed if no new listings came on the market?
>
> Let's say there's a six-month supply of homes. That's considered a balanced market, where neither buyers nor sellers have a particular advantage. During the housing boom, when housing supply in some markets fell to one or two months of inventory, competing buyers bid up prices that resulted in double-digit annual appreciation rates ("seller's market"). When inventory exceeds a six-month supply of homes, however, buyers begin to have an advantage when negotiating with competing sellers, and downward pressure on prices usually occurs ("buyer's market").

CHAPTER 2

TEAM

Selling by-owner used to mean taking on all
aspects of the marketing and negotiation
process independently — and being locked
out of the MLS. No more. Today, you have
more options.

```
┌─────────────────────────┐
│                         │
│   Shades Of FSBO        │
│                         │
└─────────────────────────┘
```

Online services: Do a quick online search with the keywords "for sale by owner" and you'll find a variety of sites that offer various types of real estate services for a fee, such as:

▶ Listing your home on the MLS and other real estate sites.

▶ Signage, fliers and advertising.

▶ Help with sales-contract preparation.

▶ Discounted agent representation.

▶ Referrals to professionals involved in getting a contract to settlement.

▶ Instructions, information and worksheets.

Remember, as a FSBO you'll want to offer a buying-side commission/fee to a real estate agent/brokerage that brings in a buyer who goes to settlement. And be sure you understand what your fees for online services are buying and how long the services are available to you.

Local discounters: *Smart Tip:* Real estate commissions are negotiable. You may find a local full-service brokerage that is willing to offer you a discount from its normal commission rate if you also hire the brokerage to help you purchase your next home. Some brokers may lower their commission just to get your listing, with the intention of offering a smaller percentage split to the selling agent/broker (but which might actually discourage them from working to find a buyer for your home).

Make sure you understand all the particulars of any discounted service you're considering. The true value of the service will be in the fine print.

TEAM

◆ ◆ ◆

Essential Takeaway

Essential Takeaway: *There is a reason why over a million people in the United States work as licensed real estate agents and join the National Association of REALTORS®... and why less than 10% of all homes are sold by-owner. Especially in a tough market, more sellers turn to agents more often to assist with their sale. Would you do surgery on yourself? No. Selling by-owner may not be surgery, but real estate today is a complex, litigious transaction that most sellers need help navigating.*

◆ ◆ ◆

Chapter 2 Roundup

Smart Essentials TEAM :: What You Have Learned

▶▶ Know the difference between agents and brokers.

▶▶ Understand what your realty commission buys.

▶▶ Use smart strategies to find the right agent.

▶▶ Avoid costly mistakes when selecting a listing agent.

▶▶ Drill into 10 smart questions before you sign a listing agreement.

▶▶ How to know when to go FSBO.

Smart Essentials

Page   **Essential Note**

_____   _____

_____   _____

_____   _____

_____   _____

_____   _____

_____   _____

_____   _____

_____   _____

_____   _____

_____   _____

_____   _____

_____   _____

_____   _____

_____   _____

_____   _____

_____   _____

_____   _____

_____   _____

_____   _____

CHAPTER 3
MONEY

In this chapter, you'll learn smart ways to:

1. Nail down your home's real market value.

2. Estimate net "walkaway cash" from your sale.

3. Find out how you can avoid capital gains taxes legally.

Despite various emotions that may be involved, selling a home is first and foremost a financial transaction — one of the biggest ones you are ever likely to make. That makes it important to crunch all the relevant numbers early in the process so you can make smart decisions as you negotiate with buyers and make plans for your next home.

Myth: *Home sellers should only focus on getting the highest price for their home.*

Not! While sale price is an important consideration, the smart focus is on the bottom line — how much money you walk away with at settlement. A number of factors go into that equation, but we'll start with finding out what your home is currently worth.

NAIL DOWN YOUR HOME'S REAL MARKET VALUE

Many sellers don't quite get how their home's value is determined by factors outside the home itself — the factors influencing the area's current real estate market. A home's value is not just about the old adage: location, location, location. It's also tied to:

🗩 **Economic conditions** that reflect both national and local business conditions, especially employment opportunities.

🗩 **Current mortgage-interest rates** and the availability of mortgage loans.

🗩 **National, state and/or local political activity** that produces changes in tax laws and tax rates, sales regulations, zoning restrictions, reassessments of property, development plans, etc.

● **Pressures of supply and demand** — the number of homes for sale in relation to the number of qualified buyers.

● **Seasonal influences** such as a "peak buying season" and "off-season."

Ultimately, though, your home's value is determined by what qualified buyers are willing to pay for it — because they are influenced by all the factors listed above. And while you only need one buyer to go to settlement, you must target the ideal subset in today's buyer pool as a *group* in order to reel in the one buyer who will purchase your home.

So how can you predict what buyers would be willing to pay for your home? You have to know what they've been paying lately.

| **Recent Sales Of Comparable Homes** |

How much have buyers paid for comparable homes[††] sold through arm's-length transactions[††] during the previous three to six months? That's the first question you'll need to answer.

[††] ***Comparable Homes***
A home is considered comparable (a "comp" in realtyspeak) by being similar in terms of location (nearby and in the same or a similar neighborhood); type (single-family, townhome, condo, etc.); size (square footage, number of rooms, bedrooms, baths); lot (size, value, location); style (colonial, contemporary, number of stories, etc.); age; and type of sale (see below).

[††] ***Arm's-Length Transactions***
Arm's-length transactions are home sales in which the buyer and seller are not related to each other and do not have common interests — they have each other at "arm's length." These are the types of sales appraisers consider when establishing the fair market value of a property. In a non-arm's-length transaction, the relationship between the parties may cause one or the other to accept less than they are entitled to or pay more than fair market value.

Examples of non-arm's-length transactions include the transfer of ownership through an estate, a sale between relatives or a company purchase of a relocating employee's home. Short sales and foreclosures are sometimes not considered by appraisers to be arm's-length transactions—and not true comparables—because their sales prices are affected by the seller's "distressed" situation, rather than the market.

On the other hand, short sales and foreclosures can still impact home values. Some researchers report as much as a 10% discount in a property's value if a foreclosure is on the market within 250 yards. Home values in areas with a significant number of short sales and foreclosures will depress your home's value, even though such sales are not true comparables.

Be aware that sales prices aren't the whole story; they don't reflect whether buyers received contributions (also called "concessions") from sellers for settlement costs, redecorating allowances, etc. For example, a home may have had a selling price of $200,000, with the sellers giving back $10,000 to the buyers at settlement—meaning the real selling value was $190,000. (More on finding accurate information shortly.)

Once you find the *real* selling prices of recent comps, you'll have a ballpark range—say, $180,000 to $220,000 based on five comps—of what today's buyers will pay for your home.

Your Home Versus Recent Comps

At this point, you may be thinking: *I've seen the comps—my home is way better! It's in primo condition and has gorgeous granite countertops.* Understandable worry. Those things count, though they may not increase your home's value quite as much as you might like.

The fact that you spent $6,000 to put granite in the kitchen doesn't necessarily mean your home is worth $6,000 more than the $200,000 comp home with Formica counters. Depending on your market, the granite might only add $4,000 of value to your home. Located on a cul-de-sac, your home could be worth 2% to 5% more than non-cul-de-sac comps. But what if you only have a single-car garage, compared with the two-car $200,000 comp? Adjustments must be made! Depending on the area, you might need to lower your home's value estimate by $3,000 to $5,000 for that one-car garage.

CHAPTER 3

MONEY

Other adjustments to value would come into play if your home has a great view, a swimming pool, built-ins, differences in flooring, ceiling heights, etc. How much each of these differences increases or decreases the value of your home will depend on the home's overall value, neighborhood standards and the region you live in.

As for condition . . . it's relative. Unless your home is in terrible shape — not just cosmetically iffy — its condition will not substantially alter its value compared with the comps. The good news: If your home is in super-great condition compared with others on the market, you'll get the most attention from buyers and sell faster than the competition.

Where To Find Information

A top-notch real estate agent has access to all the information on sales prices and listing details for comps, concessions from sellers, values associated with different home features and so on. By conducting a comparative market analysis (CMA), your agent can determine your home's market value — within a fairly narrow range compared with straight comp prices.

Finding all the relevant information is challenging on your own. You may be able to find sales-price data listed in your local newspaper, but those prices will not reflect seller concessions or property details. Another place to look for old sales prices is on your county's or city's tax-assessment database — often online but not always current. Again, no seller-compensation info. Online real estate sites[††] also estimate price information about homes, but not seller contributions.

††*Online Real Estate Sites*
A number of online sites provide easily accessible nationwide data about homes for sale, prices of homes that have sold and estimates of home values. It's information, but it's frequently not current, relevant or even accurate information.

Smart Tip: Consider spending a few hundred dollars to hire a professional real estate appraiser to evaluate your home before you put it on the market. Because appraisers have access to all the current, relevant data available, they can tell you what your home is worth in today's market. (You'll also avoid one of the costliest deal-killing mistakes in today's market — accepting a sale price higher than the appraisal and having the lender kibosh the deal. Not good when it's weeks after you thought the home was sold.)

```
Costly
Home-Valuation
Mistake To Avoid
```

Mistake: Once you've determined what your home is really worth in today's market, you can begin thinking about your listing or asking price. You may be thinking: *Why wouldn't I simply set my listing price to be the same as my home's market value?*

Solution: Your listing/asking price is a marketing tool — you can use it to attract the right buyers and fast offers. We'll dig deeper into this discussion about pricing strategies in the next chapter — it's important enough to have a whole chapter of its own!

Meanwhile, you can move ahead determining how much cash you are likely to pocket from the sale of your home.

ESTIMATE NET 'WALKAWAY CASH' FROM YOUR SALE

Knowing what your home is worth allows you to forecast how much money you'll net from your sale — your "walkaway cash." It's essential to do this calculation early in your selling process so you can make plans for your living situation after you sell your home — buying another home, paying off other debts, making investments — or for putting money on the table at settlement.

Using the market value you determined applying the information above, you want to estimate how much money you'll net after selling expenses, reimbursements and taxes (if any). Your agent can help you through the following steps.

Step 1: Start with your home's market value, then subtract any of the following items that apply:

📌 Payoff of your mortgage and any other loans backed by your home's equity. Contact your lender(s) to find the exact payoff amount — which will be different than your current mortgage balance — based on your expected settlement date.

📌 Mortgage prepayment penalty (if any). *Smart Tip:* This is usually a tax-deductible item on federal returns for the tax year in which the penalty is paid.

● **Settlement fees assigned by the contract.** These include fees normally paid by the seller, such as for a pest inspection (required in some states), services of a settlement company, etc.

● **Attorney's fees,** if any.

● **Local taxes.**

● **Real estate commissions/fees** to agents/brokers.

● **Advertising costs.** *Smart Tip:* Negotiate to have these covered by the agent/broker in the listing contract.

● **Costs to prepare your home for sale.** These could include painting, cleaning, yard services, repairs, replacements (carpet is common) and services provided by professionals such as a home stager, photographer, appraiser, home inspector (if you decide to hire your own), etc. (We'll discuss these items in Chapter 5 PREPARE.)

● **Capital gains taxes,** if any. The next section of this chapter discusses how to determine whether you'll owe capital gains taxes on any profits you make from your home.

● **Amount of seller financing.** Should you decide to offer qualified buyers a loan (second mortgage) to help them finance their purchase of your home, the loan amount would reduce the amount of cash you immediately net from your sale.

● **Carrying costs.** These are the amounts you pay for mortgage interest, insurance, taxes and maintenance between the time you put your home on the market and the time you get it sold. It's important to include these costs because each day your home stays on the market — unsold — costs you money, lowering your net walkaway cash.

Not included in the above list are contributions/concessions you make to the buyer — such as paying loan discount points[††] — because these costs should be covered by the pricing/terms strategy you develop (using information from the next chapter) in order to sell your home at its market value — the starting point of this calculation.

[††]*Loan Discount Points*
A one-time interest charge prepaid to the buyer's lender so as to lower the buyer's mortgage interest rate. Each point is 1% of the loan amount. Example: One point on a $78,000 loan is $780

($78,000 x .01 = $780). Loan discount points are paid at settlement either by the buyer or the seller—or are apportioned between them by agreement.

Sellers sometimes pay some or all discount points to attract more buyers—especially since seller-paid points paid at settlement generally can be deducted by buyers as a Schedule A mortgage expense—a double-bonus sweetener for your buyer! (Lenders may quote their price for services in points, but these charges are not tax deductible for buyers because they are not mortgage interest.)

Step 2: To the figure derived from Step 1 above, add any prepaid property taxes and insurance that will be reimbursed to you at settlement. (If your lender pays your taxes and insurance from an escrow account on your loan, ask your lender how much you would be reimbursed based on your hoped-for settlement date. Otherwise, you'll need to contact your insurance company and local taxing authority to find this information.) *Smart Tip:* If you refinanced and paid discount points that have not been fully amortized, you will realize a tax break for the balance on your sale-year tax return. *Voila!* The bottom line is your net proceeds—your walkaway cash.

Remember: Your net-proceeds computation is only a ballpark figure based on estimates. Any changes in the figures will affect your bottom line, so it's a smart idea to revisit this calculation as you go through the selling process. Why is this exercise essential? When you get an offer from a buyer, you can use the offered selling price and contract terms to recalculate your walkaway cash and evaluate the offer.

Smart Tip: As you look ahead to your after-sale life, be sure to reserve cash for the costs of moving your household goods to their new location, and expenses for improving, equipping and furnishing your next home— whether you decide to buy or rent. With some planning, you can avoid the costly mistake of being house-poor.

HOW TO AVOID CAPITAL GAINS TAXES LEGALLY

As you know from the tax deductions you've enjoyed while owning your home, housing is probably the most tax-advantaged investment available to most taxpayers. And that advantage continues through the sale of your home. Whereas profits from most other long-term investments—capital gains[††]—are subject to federal taxation upon sale at capital-gains rates, many homeowners pay no federal taxes—*zilch*—on their home-sale profits.

> ### [††] *Capital Gains*
> Capital gains are profits made on assets that have been held for more than one year. The capital gains from a home sale are not the same as the net proceeds we discussed in the section above. Instead, home-sale capital gains are the selling price minus qualified selling expenses *and* minus the "adjusted cost basis" of your home. The bottom line may be taxable, depending on the amount of gain and whether you qualify for a capital-gains exclusion. Bear in mind, even if you qualify for a federal exclusion, some states do tax home-sale capital gains—so you may not be completely off the hook.

Smart Tip: Consult IRS Publication 523, *Selling Your Home*—available at *http://www.IRS.gov*—for complete details on using the federal exclusion for home-sale capital gains.

Current Rules For Home-Sale Capital Gains

Married joint filers can exclude from taxation up to $500,000 of capital gains realized on selling a principal residence; for singles and married people filing separately, the limit is $250,000. (Gains above those limits are taxed at current capital-gains rates.) Here are the rules on qualifying for the exclusion:

● **Ownership and use test.** You must have owned and used the property as your principal residence for at least two of the five years leading up to the settlement date. Periods of ownership and use do not have to be consecutive. For example, you could live in the home six months, move to the Bahamas for two-and-a-half years, then move back to the home and live in it for another one-and-a-half years before selling it.

● **Two-year test.** You cannot have used the exclusion in the previous two years—or, simply put, you can use the exclusion as often as every two years.

CHAPTER 3

MONEY

● **Reduced exclusion.** You may qualify for a reduced exclusion if you do not meet the ownership-and-use tests, or you fail the two-year test *and* the main reason for selling your home was due to a qualified change in place of employment, qualified health issue or qualified unforeseen circumstance. Such issues could earn you an exclusion as a pro-rated percentage of two years.

● **Mixed-use Rule.** Just so you know, the Housing and Economic Recovery Act of 2008 changed the treatment of capital gains from the sale of a home that the owners sometimes used as a principal residence and sometimes used as a second home or rental property. Gains attributable to the period of second-home or rental use ("non-qualified use") on or after January 1, 2009 are taxable at capital-gains rates, while gains attributable to principal-residence use may be excluded up to the $500,000 or $250,000 limits, providing ownership and use tests are met. *Smart Tip:* This costly mistake sometimes trips up Baby Boomers who were planning to retire to their second home but changed their minds and sold the second home instead.

● **Surviving spouse rule.** Surviving spouses may exclude gains up to $500,000 for a principal residence jointly owned with the deceased spouse, provided the property is sold or exchanged within two years of the spouse's death and standard ownership and use tests are met.

● **Rule for uniformed services, Foreign Service, intelligence community and Peace Corps.** Personnel of these organizations who serve a period of "qualified official extended duty" can suspend the five-year ownership/use test period for the length of that duty up to 10 years.

Compute Your Gains

If you know you'll qualify for the $500,000 or $250,000 exclusion and the profit from your home sale is likely to be well under the limit that applies, skip forward to the next chapter. If, on the other hand, your profit is likely to be close to or above your limit, use the following information to determine whether you'll owe capital-gains taxes on your sale.

Step 1. Calculate the amount you're likely to realize from the sale. For IRS purposes, this is the total amount you receive for your home — its sale price — minus your selling expenses, which may include such items as commissions, advertising fees, legal fees, inspections and loan charges that you pay. *Smart Tip:* Some of the selling expenses you used to calculate net proceeds may not be allowed as qualified expenses when computing capital gains; see IRS Publication 523, *Selling Your Home,* for a complete list of qualified selling expenses.

Step 2. Compute your home's "cost basis." The cost basis of your home is the purchase price you originally paid for it plus certain acquisition and settlement costs. Adding these costs to the purchase price increases the "basis" of your home, thereby lowering your profit and liability for capital-gains taxes. Qualified settlement and acquisition costs include:

- ► Loan application fees
- ► Inspection costs
- ► Appraisal fees
- ► Credit-report costs
- ► Loan discount fees
- ► Assumption fees
- ► Transfer taxes
- ► Removal-of-liens fees
- ► Title search fees
- ► Title insurance fees
- ► Recording fees
- ► Document preparation fees
- ► Legal fees
- ► Mandated repair costs
- ► Home-search expenses (including qualified travel)

Smart Tip: Most of the above costs are shown on the settlement statement ("HUD-1") for your home purchase. (You did save it, didn't you? If not, contact the company or attorney who handled the settlement to request a copy.)

Step 3. Adjust the basis. Certain items increase or decrease your home's basis. Costs for items such as the following should be added to the cost basis from Step 2:

● Additions and other improvements that have a useful life of more than one year. (Repairs and maintenance expenses do not qualify.)

- Special assessments for local improvements.

- Amounts spent to restore damage after a casualty loss.

Be sure to *subtract* from your home's basis amounts for items such as insurance payments received for a casualty loss, payments received for granting an easement or any gain you postponed from the sale of a previous home before May 7, 1997. Again, IRS Publication 523 has all the info.

Step 4. Subtract. Finally, subtract your adjusted basis (Step 3) from the amount realized from the sale (Step 1). If the answer is a positive number, you have capital gains; if negative, a capital loss. Remember, you will only owe taxes on the amount above the exclusion limit you qualify for — $500,000 or $250,000 or a reduced exclusion — assuming you do qualify for an exclusion. Capital-gains taxes, if owed, must be paid with the tax return (on Form 1040, Schedule D) for the year the home is sold. For planning purposes, do a quick search online to find out the current capital-gains tax rate and how your income may affect your rate.

Smart Tip: If your gains are larger than the exclusion amounts — or you don't qualify for an exclusion — you can reduce your immediate tax burden by making an installment sale,[††] spreading out your gain from the property — and your taxes — over a period of years. If you converted your home to an investment/rental property, you might be able to use a Section 1031 exchange or "tax-free swap" to defer the gains into another investment property. Consult your tax professional for help negotiating the complexities of these options.

> [††] *Installment Sale*
> An installment sale, according to the IRS, is a sale in which part or all of the sale price is paid in a later year or years. Practically speaking, it means you become your buyer's lender, allowing the buyer to purchase your home over time — according to the details of your contract.

Now that you have all the important numbers lined up, you can move on to perhaps the most important exercise in the process of getting your home sold — *setting the right listing price.* Listing price is so important we've given it the entire next chapter.

Chapter 3 Roundup

Smart Essentials MONEY :: What You Have Learned

▶▶ How to determine your home's real market value.

▶▶ How to evaluate your home compared with recent comps.

▶▶ What information to look for and where to find it.

▶▶ Key steps to estimating your walkaway cash.

▶▶ How to avoid capital-gains taxes legally.

▶▶ Four steps to compute your capital gains.

CHAPTER 4

PRICE

In this chapter, you'll learn smart ways to:

1. Use your asking price as a marketing tool.

2. Avoid overpricing your home.

3. Set a "strategic" listing price.

USE YOUR ASKING PRICE AS A MARKETING TOOL

If there were an eighth wonder of the marketing world, we'd nominate your home's listing price (or *asking* price if you're selling FSBO) as your most important tool. That said, let's be serious: Guesstimates don't fly — you need actual facts and data to properly *position your home in your local market.*

Hopefully, you've already determined your home's current market value — within a tightly defined range — using the information in Chapter 3. And, of course, you want to sell your home at the top end of its value range if at all possible. A less-sophisticated seller would simply use that top-end value as the listing price and hope for the best. Smart sellers know there is a better way.

◆ ◆ ◆

Essential Takeaway

Essential Takeaway: The major factor that determines your home's market value is what other comparable homes have recently sold for. The essential secret to setting a smart listing price is to determine what other comparable homes on the market are currently listed for — and position your price to stand out from the crowd. Simply said: Price sells.

◆ ◆ ◆

No home sale occurs in a vacuum—you have competition! The competition is all the other homes like yours that are looking for a willing and able buyer to make an offer. And since price is one of the first factors considered by the vast majority of buyers—who are limited in number—you need to set your price so buyers flock to your home, not the competition's.

Take A Buyer's Perspective

To effectively use your listing price as a marketing tool, you must understand how buyers view price:

💬 A well-priced home attracts buyer interest (though once you have their interest, they'll be more concerned about whether they can afford the monthly mortgage payment than about price).

💬 Most buyers have decided where they want to live and have shopped the competition in the neighborhood with a knowledgeable real estate agent. Buyers know how your home compares.

💬 All buyers want to cash in on a good deal.

💬 Buyers recognize value and shy away from overpriced homes.

💬 Buyers don't want to pay for your mistakes (paying too much when you purchased, over-improving the home, poor-quality or over-the-top remodeling jobs, etc.).

💬 Buyers have no interest in how much money you need to realize from the sale to make your next move.

◆ ◆ ◆

Essential Takeaway

Essential Takeaway: *The right price for your home is the one that will attract the most attention from buyers, putting you in a position to negotiate the sales contract to your advantage.*

◆ ◆ ◆

AVOID OVERPRICING YOUR HOME

The right listing price for a home is usually within 5% of its current market value and usually results in a fair-dollar sale within a reasonable amount of time. But if prices are declining in your home's real estate market, even 5% above market value is overpricing.

You may be tempted to set your home's price higher than its value — and higher than the listing prices of other comps on the market — so you have more room to negotiate with buyers. Or you may hope some buyer who isn't familiar with your local market will fall in love with your home and offer to pay your too-high price out of ignorance. Or you may think that a higher price than other similar homes can be justified by your excellent decorating. Think again.

Any experienced agent will tell you that setting a too-high listing price will come back to bite you. They're not just saying that to collect a quick sales commission. (After all, the more your home sells for, the higher their compensation from the sale.) Top-notch agents know that overpricing rarely gets a home sold for the best possible price and contract terms. (We'll talk more about contract terms as part of pricing later in this chapter.)

◆ ◆ ◆

Essential Takeaway

Essential Takeaway: *The period of best opportunity for selling a home at its market value is the first four weeks after it goes on the market. That's when buyers who have seen most available listings are waiting for just the right home to come along. If your home is priced right from the start, you are in the best position to attract the maximum number of buyers able to pay the price your home is worth — and to sell your home within your timetable.*

◆ ◆ ◆

Here's why overpricing does not work:

● **Buyers may simply ignore your home** because they have already found better values elsewhere. Your overpriced home makes other homes look more attractive — helping them sell first. (We call this the "Cream Principle."[††])

[††] ***Cream Principle***

Every month the best properties sell — those with the best price, best condition, best terms, best location. They are the "cream" homes that rise above the other homes for sale and are snapped up by serious buyers who recognize value.

Unfortunately, waiting one's turn for "cream" properties to sell first rarely works, because new listings constantly enter the market. These new homes for sale typically have prices based on what sold in the previous month (or months) — and they are positioned to beat the unsold properties and expired listings that buyers have already skipped over.

● **A too-high price eliminates a whole class of buyers.** Many buyers know just how high they can go and don't even look at homes priced above their ceiling.

● **A buyer willing to pay an over-market price may not be able to get financing.** Lenders often reject loan applications when the home's appraisal comes back lower than the contract price. The delay from a failed sale can mean you waste the crucial first-30-days marketing period.

● **Every day your home remains unsold as you wait for a too-high price adds to your carrying costs** — amounts you pay for mortgage interest, taxes, insurance and maintenance. In effect, you're spending money in hopes of getting a price buyers are unlikely to pay. As we showed in Chapter 3, it's not the sale price that counts. Your focus should be on the bottom line — your net proceeds.

● **You waste time** and suffer added weeks or months of stress as your overpriced home languishes on the market, preventing you from moving on to your next home.

● **Your unsold home may eventually be seen as "stale inventory,"** suggesting to buyers that it has structural or mechanical shortcomings, even though it doesn't.

🗩 **After a long time on the market, you'll have to lower your price below market value** just to revive buyers' attention—losing money compared with what you would have gotten had you priced right from the start.

SET A 'STRATEGIC' LISTING PRICE

Strategic pricing means setting a smart listing price that accomplishes two essential objectives:

1. Attracting buyers' attention so they'll take a close look at your property and make an offer to purchase it.

2. Selling your home at its true market value.

◆ ◆ ◆

Essential Takeaway

Essential Takeaway: Your listing price is just a starting point. Once an interested buyer makes a purchase offer, you negotiate the details of the contract to get a market-value sale and the bottom-line proceeds you're looking for.

◆ ◆ ◆

As we've said before, buyers will pay attention to the best values on the market in their price range. And they'll make offers on homes that provide what they're looking for at the best price and terms. That means your listing price must beat or at least equal that of your competition—taking into account the amenities your home offers compared with the competition.

Eight Really Smart Price Strategies

There could be several "right" prices for your home, depending on the contract terms you're willing to offer buyers, available financing options, your home's condition and market trends. Here are some smart strategies to consider.

PRICE

Smart strategy #1: Underprice for fast offers. Setting a price below market value isn't usually the best approach because, obviously, you could end up losing thousands of dollars on one of your major investments. In some situations, however, underpricing can work to your advantage.

If time is more important than money and you need a faster-than-average sale, you might consider setting a bargain price to attract the greatest number of prospects and fast offers. Why? You're willing to trade money for a quick settlement.

A lower-than-market price could also result in a number of qualified buyers launching a bidding war that auctions your sale price up to where the listing price should have been in the first place — perhaps even higher. This "low starting price" strategy lets the market set the price of your home. Advertise the home. Show the home. Take initial bids. Ask for final bids. Sell to the highest bidder — or not. *Smart Tip:* You don't have to accept any price that's offered.

This may be a difficult strategy to pull off without a real estate agent at your side to generate buyer traffic through other agents and handle the negotiations. And remember, there's no guarantee buyers will end up fighting to win your sales contract, so consider this price-setting strategy carefully.

Smart strategy #2: Price with a seller contribution.[††] A big hurdle for many buyers is coming up with enough cash for the down payment and settlement costs. Solve that problem by specifying in your listing that you're willing to contribute, say, $6,000 or x% of the sale price toward the buyer's settlement costs — then increase your listing price by the same amount — or not.

[††] ***Seller Contribution***
A seller contribution is an agreement by the seller to contribute cash to the buyer at settlement to pay for items such as loan discount points, appraisal fees, legal costs, transfer recording fees and prepaid or escrow items such as real estate taxes and homeowners insurance.

Lenders limit the amount of seller contributions. Contribution caps vary by lender, but typically range from 3% to 6% of the home's sale price or market value.

PRICE

Bear in mind, your price must still be competitive with that of comparable homes on the market so as not to dampen interest in your home. Rather than including a seller contribution in your listing, you could instead save the offer as a "closer" to use in negotiations with your buyer.

Smart strategy #3: Price for a loan assumption.[††] Do you have an assumable mortgage at an interest rate lower than current market rates? If so, you can help buyers solve another common problem — securing an affordable mortgage. Many a buyer would be happy to pay a somewhat higher price for your home in order to get your lower-interest mortgage and a lower monthly payment. In addition, a loan assumption may cost the buyer less than paying settlement costs for a new mortgage. Be sure to learn your lender's requirements before offering a loan assumption to potential buyers.

> [††] *Loan Assumption*
>
> Some mortgage loans are assumable, that is, they can be transferred to another person. In most cases, loan assumptions require lender approval, ensuring that the new borrower meets the lender's qualifications. Usually, the buyer becomes responsible for all remaining payments on the loan, according to the original loan terms. In addition, the buyer must make arrangements to pay for the seller's equity — either with cash, through a second loan (from a lender or the seller) or using some combination of the two. The seller may or may not be released from liability for the loan, depending on the lender.
>
> Mortgages with a "due-on-sale clause" must be paid off when the home is sold and thus are not usually assumable. Some lenders, however, may allow the assumption of due-on-sale loans with restructured terms, such as a higher interest rate — not something that would interest many buyers.

Smart strategy #4: Price with financing. Offering to finance some or all of a buyer's mortgage can justify a price toward the higher end of your home's value. Many buyers lack enough cash to handle the hefty down-payment requirements of today's mortgage loans. You could offer to finance part of a buyer's 20% down payment — say 10% — assuming the buyer's lender goes along with the deal.

If you do not need or want cash immediately from your home sale, but would prefer a stream of income from the property, you might consider financing the entire sale price. In effect, you become your buyer's lender.

These types of arrangements do not come without risk, particularly from buyer default. Take extra care to ensure the creditworthiness of your buyer and use the expertise of a knowledgeable real estate attorney to draw up a contract that strongly protects your financial interests.

Smart strategy #5: Price ahead of the market. Not setting a price that anticipates price trends in an unstable market — where prices are increasing or decreasing rapidly — is a bad idea. Smart sellers know their home's value can change from one day to the next. In these situations, it pays to price ahead of the market.

Let's say sales prices for homes comparable to yours have been steadily increasing over the past several quarters. To take advantage of the trend, you can price your home, say, 3% higher than its current calculated market value. This strategy doesn't count as overpricing because you know the demand is there. By the time you get an offer and negotiate a contract with a buyer, other home sales will have closed at higher prices, resulting in an appraisal that supports your higher price.

Pricing ahead of the market is also smart in situations where sales prices of comparable homes have been steadily falling. To ensure that your home captures buyer attention fast, you can set your price perhaps 3% lower than the low end of its current value range and that of other comparable homes. The saving grace is this strategy prevents you from having to make constant price reductions as home values continue to drop. It also helps ensure that the appraisal ordered by your buyer's lender will support your contract price.

Smart strategy #6: Price for remodelers. If your home's condition is dated compared with similar homes in your neighborhood, you have two choices: Spend money to update your home or lower your price to invite interest.

It makes sense (remember the "Cream Principle") to invest a small amount of money to make sure your home looks clean and fresh at showings. But spending a lot of money to add granite countertops or hardwood floors, remodel bathrooms and kitchens, etc., isn't likely to boost your home's value enough to recover those expenses.

CHAPTER 4

PRICE

Consider pricing your home at the bottom of its value range and lower than other comps on the market. The price alone will attract immediate attention. And as long as your home is move-in ready, buyers who want things their way will see the value in being able to remodel the home according to their own tastes and priorities. The money they save buying your lower-priced home can pay for the upgrades they really want.

Another smart idea: Price toward the higher end of the value range but offer a remodeling or redecorating allowance to be paid to the buyer at settlement.

Smart strategy #7: Avoid rounding. Set a precise listing price. Researchers at Cornell University report that people will pay more for a home with a listing price that does not end in all zeros. They said that comparing a list price of $485,000 with a price of $484,700, the second more-precise price would ultimately sell for about $1,380 more, on average, than the more-rounded figure.

Because of what the researchers describe as a "bias in judgment," home buyers tend to perceive a price as being smaller when it ends in numbers other than zeros — the fewer zeros, the better. The study attributed the bias to the fact that people are accustomed to precise numbers for low-cost items (e.g., $4.99 for an eBook) and to rounded numbers for high-cost items.

Of course, it shades toward the ridiculous to price a home at, say, $325,231, but $325,250 would answer the call just fine.

Smart strategy #8: Get under the break point. If your home's value is close to a numerical break point — say $225,000 — price under it — say, $224,950. The reasons are simple:

1. Buyers think about home prices in terms of numerical break points: "We can't go over $210,000, but let's look up to $225,000 and maybe we can negotiate down."

2. When searching online, preset price ranges on drop-down menus won't return a property priced just over the max range a buyer has selected.

3. Buyers tend to focus on the first part of a large number. Although $224,950 is only $50 less than $225,000, many buyers will tend to remember the number as being closer to $224,000.

Costly Pricing Mistakes To Avoid

Mistake #1: Swimming against the stream of the market. Sellers, understandably, want to get the most for their home and typically think their "unique" home is better than other nearby properties. Going against the psychology of the market is a short road to a long sale.

Solution: Before you put your home on the market, shop for a home like yours. Go to open houses. Visit model homes. Tour homes online. Drive by homes for sale from a list your agent provides from the MLS. Turn your mindset from selling "your home" to selling real estate; selling a property; selling a thing. Once you see how the market is flowing, you can make the market currents work for you . . . not against you.

Mistake #2: Playing cowboy. For owners who think they've got their fingertips on the pulse of their neighborhood, it is tempting to ignore a seasoned agent's advice about pricing. Or worse, listen instead to a neighbor or barber or cousin.

Solution: If you've found a top agent you trust, pay attention to what he or she is telling you about pricing your home. Nothing can cost you more in the complex, litigious, money-pit maze of home selling like not taking the advice of an experienced pro. Don't be a cowboy; let your pro watch out for your best interests.

By now, you should have a pretty clear idea of the best listing price for your home. But price alone will not sell your home. In Chapter 5 PREPARE, we'll discuss essential techniques to prepare your home to reel in the best purchase offer.

Chapter 4 Roundup

Smart Essentials PRICE :: What You Have Learned

▶▶ Positioning your home's price is a major marketing tool.

▶▶ Look at your home sale from a buyer's perspective.

▶▶ Overpricing won't help your bottom-line proceeds.

▶▶ *Smart strategy #1:* Underprice for fast offers.

▶▶ *Smart strategy #2:* Price with a seller contribution.

▶▶ *Smart strategy #3:* Price for a loan assumption.

▶▶ *Smart strategy #4:* Price with financing.

▶▶ *Smart strategy #5:* Price ahead of the market.

▶▶ *Smart strategy #6:* Price for remodelers.

▶▶ *Smart strategy #7:* Avoid rounding.

▶▶ *Smart strategy #8:* Get under the break point.

▶▶ Avoid pricing mistakes like the plague!

Smart Essentials

Page	Essential Note
_____	_____
_____	_____
_____	_____
_____	_____
_____	_____
_____	_____
_____	_____
_____	_____
_____	_____
_____	_____
_____	_____
_____	_____
_____	_____
_____	_____
_____	_____
_____	_____
_____	_____
_____	_____
_____	_____

PREPARE

In this chapter, you'll learn smart ways to:

1. Create "Stop the car, Honey!" curb appeal.

2. Put your home into move-in condition.

3. Stage your home to sell faster with "Wow!" factor and photos.

Getting your home in tip-top shape is of utmost importance before putting it on the market for the world to see. That means focusing on curb appeal, condition, staging and photography. Once you've perfected these elements, you'll be ready for show time!

CREATE 'STOP THE CAR, HONEY!' CURB APPEAL

The exterior of a home and the grounds surrounding it create a strong first impression on home buyers. If a property shows shoddy upkeep, faded paint and unattractive landscaping, buyers viewing it online or from the curb will likely assume more shabbiness inside. They won't even go there unless, of course, they're looking for a bargain-priced fixer-upper.

Pretend you're shopping for a home with a notebook and an attitude. Look at your property critically from the street, as a buyer would, and walk slowly closer, jotting down what you notice along the way — overgrown shrubbery, weeds, a crooked shutter, driveway cracks, etc. Make note of anything you see that needs repairs, trimming, removal or replacement. *Smart Tip:* Take a look at your home after dark, too. Many busy home buyers use weekday evenings to drive by homes and weekend days to visit them. Does your home look bright and inviting? Can you read the house numbers?

Cut to the chase: The overall impression your home makes is really a composite of six essentials. Focus on each element individually to create an attractive "buy now" first impression of your home.

● **Location:** Short of picking up and moving your home to another lot, the only thing you can do about its location is emphasize the good points and minimize any bad ones. For example, if your home sits on a corner lot, you may want to install an attractive hedge or fence to create more privacy in the exposed side yard. That's also a useful approach if a neighbor's lot is an eyesore.

● **Architecture:** Here's how to punch up your home's style. Select a slightly contrasting paint color that coordinates with the color of the home to emphasize special features such as columns, trim, porches, shutters, doors, and so on. Less-attractive features, such as gutter downspouts, can be painted the same color as the home so they blend in. On the right home, the addition of window shutters can add interest, as would a porch railing, decorative picket fence or lattice panels to screen an open area under steps, deck or porch.

● **Landscaping:** If your lawn and garden look helter-skelter, ask a local nursery to draw up a remodeling plan to make best use of what's already there. Add new plants, trees or shrubs, as needed. You can do the work yourself or hire a landscaper to make changes for you.

Remember, plantings should frame rather than dominate the home. Remove old shrubs and trees that have overgrown their location, no longer look healthy or block a view of doors, windows or walkways. Substitute mulch in hard-to-mow locations. Make sure flowerbeds and lawn are cut, edged, weeded and watered while your home is on the market.

Smart Tip: Your single most-important home photo is the front, exterior (what Mad Men call your "brand shot"). This picture is seen first, and in many ads it will be the only photo. It needs as much "Wow!" as possible, especially for buyers online. Create your landscape plan for an unobstructed view of your home with this signature photo in mind.

● **Details.** Mailboxes, house numbers, screens, light fixtures, railings, front door finish, doorknocker, handles and kick plates can adorn a home or detract from it. Make sure exterior hardware is properly installed, operable, attractive and in good condition. Think about adding floodlights or pathway lighting to show off your home after dark. (Be conservative, though; too many path lights, especially in a straight line, can look like an airport landing strip.)

● **Upkeep.** The most important impression you want your home to convey is that it is clean and well-maintained. First, minimize or do away with yard clutter — lawn ornaments (goodbye garden gnomes, flamingos), grills, furniture, yard tools, garbage cans and toys. Remove extra vehicles, boats, RVs. *Smart Tip:* Don't fill up your garage or carport with these items — store them in a shed, if available, or rent off-property storage for items you can't part with.

Fill any driveway cracks and apply a fresh coat of sealer. Invest in a fresh paint job that fits both the home and the neighborhood.

Pressure wash your home's siding, brick and deck. Power washers are also great for removing stains and mold from patios, driveways and walkways. Use a chemical compound if your roof shows mold patches or streaks. Apply a grease remover to the carport or garage floor. Clean the windows!

● **Extra pizzazz:** Add interest to just two or three areas outside your home using a decorative planter or potted flowers, distinctive mailbox, welcome mat, seasonal banner, window boxes, front-porch swing, garden bench or bird bath. Stage the outside for the view from inside.

PUT YOUR HOME IN JUST-RIGHT CONDITION

Make sure everything inside your home is in good working order. One way to check your home's "just right" condition is to hire a professional home inspector. For a few hundred dollars, a professional inspector will take a good look at your home, inside and out, identifying anything that isn't quite up to snuff — problems with the roof, electrical system, plumbing, heating/AC, appliances, foundation, walls/ceilings and so on. *Smart Tip:* Most buyers will order a professional inspection of your home either before making an offer or as a contingency in their contract. By hiring your own inspector before listing, you can remedy any identified issues to help ensure they won't become problems you have to negotiate with your buyers later — slowing or threatening your sale.

Even if you don't hire your own inspector, you can go through your home, room by room, looking for issues. Open everything; buyers will. Here are some items to be aware of — and to replace or repair as needed:

▶ Doors and drawers
▶ Electric switches and outlets
▶ Plumbing
▶ Heating/AC
▶ Appliances

▶ Ceilings and walls
▶ Floors
▶ Roof/attic
▶ Foundation

Costly Condition Mistakes To Avoid

Mistake #1: Not seeing defects that buyers consider deal killers. You may no longer notice the leaky faucets, squeaky doors, stained carpet, pet scratches, overstuffed closets, etc., in your home. These types of defects, however, are deal killers to buyers who want to buy a dream, not a nightmare.

Solution: Get professional opinions. Top agents look at homes the way buyers do. If you don't use a professional stager, consider paying for tips from an interior designer. *Smart Tip:* As you begin to think of your home as a "house," you'll begin to detach emotionally. Your home becomes a real estate asset — a commodity to sell.

Mistake #2: Spending too much on major home renovations. Making the wrong changes, wasting time and money that you won't recoup is bad enough. In the worst case, you could prolong the sale and have to reduce your ultimate sale price because you weren't ready for the highest-buyer-interest first days on the market.

Solution: Sometimes improvements are needed if your property won't pass muster for a home inspection or appraisal. Definitely fix the roof or foundation or pest damage — whatever is required. In other cases, improvements are needed to match the quality of competing listings or when one room doesn't match others (think old wallpaper, paint or carpet). Improvements do pay if they increase value, like making a half bath a full one. Remember, though, worthwhile improvements are those that buyers can see, such as new flooring or countertops, rather than items like insulation or Internet wiring. *Smart Tip:* Skip costly improvements and reflect the true condition in your listing price, or give buyers cash at settlement (if needed).

CLEAN, CLEAN, CLEAN

If you do nothing else to get your home ready to sell, make sure it gets a meticulous cleaning before the photo shoot and before it goes on the market. Then be sure it stays immaculate until you've secured a sales contract.

If you don't have the time and attention-to-detail needed to render your home spotless, invest in a professional cleaning service that can get the initial job done in short order. Have the windows professionally washed, too.

◆ ◆ ◆

Essential Takeaway

Essential Takeaway: Your home must not only be clean, it must also look clean.

◆ ◆ ◆

If you can't remove marks on walls and woodwork, consider touching up or repainting the entire area. If caulking can't be bleached white, remove it and replace it. Carpeting that can't be cleaned of spots and odors should be replaced (you don't have to go high-end; builder-grade will do the job well enough at a lower cost).

Be particularly aware of odors. Pets, tobacco smoke, mildew and preparation of certain foods leave behind smells that buyers will notice immediately. Room deodorizers and sprays that mask can be red flags. Removal and/or replacement of soft furnishings — carpets and pads, curtains, drapes, etc. — may be necessary to eliminate some odors. Plan for a good cleaning every week and interim cleanings daily while on the market.

STAGE TO SELL FASTER WITH 'WOW!' FACTOR AND PHOTOS

The idea of staging is to create a look that allows buyers to move in mentally—to envision themselves living in the home. Proper staging can dramatically improve the prospects of a home sale.

Not sure what a staged home should look like? New-home builders spend thousands of dollars decorating their models to elicit an emotional response from potential buyers. You won't see the things we live with daily—a ragged front-door mat, the magazine rack with last week's papers, photos and magnets on the refrigerator, toothbrushes and personal hygiene items in bathrooms, etc. Model homes look like what we would want our homes to look like if we could keep life and all our stuff neatly under control.

Staging uses what is already in your home to highlight the assets and functionality of each space. You can and should make small, affordable changes that will make your home roomy, bright, up-to-date, functional and neutral in color. (If you plan to make some of the changes suggested below, do so before the big cleaning suggested above.)

Here are some essential secrets home stagers rely on:

● **Create a well-maintained, inviting exterior** — in essence, curb appeal (covered earlier).

● **De-clutter.** Pare down visible possessions — furniture, knick-knacks, decorations, countertop items, plug-in appliances — to bare minimum. Remove photographs and personal things that mark the home as yours. Same goes for religious, political or ideological items. Put away pet bowls and litter boxes. De-clutter to the point where rooms feel somewhat empty and traffic flows easily through each room. Ultimately, you are simply packing early.

Free your closets (reduce clothes to half and make floor visible), cupboards, cabinets and storage spaces of anything you don't use on a daily or weekly basis. Store off-season items elsewhere. Stow half your books away. If you can't bring yourself to donate, sell or toss stuff, put it in temporary storage at an off-site location.

CHAPTER 5

PREPARE

❖ ❖ ❖

Essential Takeaway

Essential Takeaway: *You're not selling your things or your sense of decor; you're selling your space, and that's what buyers need to feel part of. Your personal items will get in the way of buyers visualizing your home as theirs.*

❖ ❖ ❖

● **Define each room for a single function.** Take the exercise equipment out of the family room or bedroom. Put toy chests in children's rooms, not the living room. Eat-in kitchens should sport a dinette set. Place attractive table-settings on your dining-room table to show off its usability. In greatrooms that are supposed to have more than one function, use an area rug to help define one function of the room from another. If you use a bedroom as an office or craft room, turn it back into a bedroom, so your three-bedroom place doesn't show like a two-bedroom. In short, demonstrate to buyers how each room in your home can contribute to a comfortable living environment.

● **Repaint rooms in modern, neutral colors** if you've indulged your urge for drama and "uniqueness" with eclectic paint colors over the years. That doesn't mean every room has to be beige or off-white — two safe choices, though. Lighter shades of gray, blue, yellow, green and brown tones can work.

❖ ❖ ❖

Essential Takeaway

Essential Takeaway: *Among the most-affordable improvements you can make, fresh paint offers the advantage of making walls look bright and clean. As the pros say, buyers love the smell of fresh paint. If you're having trouble picking paint, good local paint stores employ color consultants who will steer you in the right direction.*

❖ ❖ ❖

● **Create views with a room.** Doorways are where visitors get their first impression of each room in your home. Make changes to rooms — furniture arrangements, artwork placement, etc. — based on what you see from the door leading in.

● **Arrange furniture to enhance space.** Place couches, chairs and tables so they don't impede traffic through the room or from one room to another. If room size allows, create visual interest by arranging furniture grouping and rugs at an angle to the walls.

● **Maximize light.** Ditch the heavy drapes for lighter-weight curtains, sheers or blinds, or let the windows speak for themselves. Where privacy is not a concern, sparkling-clean windows can look great with a simple cornice board or valence — or no treatment at all. Ensure each room has adequate lighting — lamps, task lighting, etc.

● **Balance hard and soft surfaces.** Too many hard surfaces — flooring, wood furniture, tile, countertops, shutters, cabinets, etc. — make a space feel cold. Too many soft surfaces — upholstered items, carpets and rugs, draperies, pillows, throws, linens — create a smaller feel.

● **Arrange by ones or threes.** A single item on a small table top is sufficient, while three complementary items arranged together in a triangle add interest. Going beyond three items risks a cluttered look, especially in the kitchen. Pack away almost everything from countertops.

● **Minimize artwork.** Strike a balance between empty walls and too much artwork. Wall art should accent furniture arrangements and decor rather than attract buyers' attention. Large walls can be a problem; consider using a large, nicely framed mirror or an arrangement of similarly framed art works. Steer clear of artwork that might make some viewers uncomfortable.

● **Remove wallpaper** unless it is integral to the architecture of your home (think Victorian). Wallpaper tends to be furnishing-specific; if buyers don't like your choice, they'll see your wallpaper as a huge, messy, labor-intensive project they'd just as soon avoid.

● **Display your best matching towels in bathrooms,** or purchase new ones. Consider replacing shower curtains and remove area rugs to feature tile.

PREPARE

🖝 **Replace outdated fixtures.** New hardware for kitchen and bath cupboards can change the whole look of a room. Giving cabinets a facelift with new doors can be a dramatically economical kitchen makeover. Update lighting fixtures.

🖝 **Maximize storage** by attacking attic, basement, garage and garden shed. Clean it, organize it, store it, stack it, get rid of it. Sweep out debris, dead insects, mice droppings, etc. Buyers who see crammed storage spaces will likely conclude that your home lacks adequate storage—not that you have too much stuff!

Costly Staging Mistakes To Avoid	**Mistake #1: Deciding to do-it-yourself because a professional stager costs too much.** Just remember, for every month it takes to sell your home, that's one more month of carrying costs you didn't need to

pay . . . and in the meantime, somebody else may buy the dream home you intended to buy after your sale.

Solution: If the homestead needs more than de-personalizing, de-cluttering, de-dirting, hire a pro. Here are six tips:

1. Ask agents and friends for referrals to stagers.
2. Visit their websites — pour over before-and-after photos and case histories.
3. Determine whether the stager has experience knowing local buyers' tastes and preferences.
4. Expect a top-notch resale stager to produce a room-by-room makeover plan. (If you're really pinched, pay for just the plan, then you and your agent pick what to change.)
5. Be sure the stager has liability insurance for injury on your job.
6. Expect fees to range from a few hundred dollars for a "plan only" fee up to 1% to 1.5% of the sale price if the stager performs substantial tasks and arranges rental furniture. Larger or vacant properties cost more.

Smart Tip: Stagers have resources from photo-shoot props to furniture rentals, and they know suppliers from handymen to landscapers. Just don't expect the stager to be your general contractor and oversee improvement projects. Also, get clear on where their staging stops and your organizing, packing and moving begins.

Mistake #2: Confusing normal home decorating with staging to sell. Case in point: Some homeowners balk at pulling their coffee maker out of the cabinet every morning or wonder what they will wear with half their clothes packed away. These owners make the costly mistake of thinking staging is about them.

Solution: Staging, like retail merchandising, is about selling faster. Your stuff is not the star. Your house is the star. Avoid the costly mistake of expecting buyers to see past your stuff to see themselves at home. Eliminate distractions. Strive for "Wow!"

PLAN YOUR PHOTO SHOOT TO BEAT THE COMPETITION

Once you've staged your home's desirable features to the nines, you'll need outstanding photos for use online and in printed materials. The purpose of these pictures is to compel serious buyers to see more — in person. Photos are so crucial, we recommend you hire a pro, but if you or your agent is a great photographer, go for it!

🔴 **24/7 open house.** The primary purpose of great photos is to create a 24/7 open house online. Still photos, sometimes accompanied by music or narrative, make great slide shows for your online listing. *Smart Tip:* Ten great photos are better than 45 bad ones.

🔴 **Brand shot.** Look for the best angle to take pictures of your home's exterior. A full-frontal view may not necessarily be the best choice. Think about capturing both the front and side of the home — especially if the side shows a nice architectural feature. Shooting with the sun at your back will make this essential photo pop.

🔴 **Back yard.** Other exterior photo opportunities might include a patio, deck, pergola, garage or other architectural asset. Consider a shot at dusk if outside lighting and glowing windows show off the home well. If you have a great view, be sure to include a photo of it.

🔴 **Location.** Include photos of sought-after amenities in your neighborhood or nearby, such as a subdivision sign, school, shopping, playground, tree-lined street, farmers market, public transit, nearby college or park. Sell your location through photos.

● **Lights, action.** If you don't have enough lighting, time your indoor photo shoot carefully, taking pictures when sunshine is pouring in through windows and skylights. (Dark rooms turn off buyers.) You might have to shoot in two or three sessions to get each room pictured at its daytime-light peak. Shoot from the long angle to make rooms look larger.

● **Close-ups.** Don't bother taking photos of areas that will not help sell your home — out-of-date bathrooms, for example. Do, however, include room focal points such as fireplaces, kitchen islands, large windows and other special features that buyers value.

● **Enhance.** When you've made your photo selection, enhance photos with computer software to sharpen, lighten and make images pop off the screen (but avoid the temptation to materially alter reality).

Costly Photography Mistake To Avoid

Mistake: Using listing photos that drive away traffic. Almost 90% of buyers today begin their home search online, according to National Association of REALTORS® research. What buyers want is pictures, lots of pictures. In the Internet age, some buyers lack the attention span to read text. If your photos don't make the first cut online, the home won't even earn a drive-by.

Solution: Again, hire a real estate photographer specialist. A study of listing photos by Redfin, a Seattle-based brokerage, found that almost 85% of listings featured lower-end point-and-shoot camera photography, rather than high-quality photos. Great photography of a well-staged home sets great expectations and maximizes traffic.

One Last Selling Mistake To Avoid

Mistake: Thinking cleanups, fix-ups, staging and photography are a magic wand.

Solution: Preparing your home for sale and staging are not a substitute for proper pricing. As the saying goes, you can dress up a pig but you still have a pig. Few buyers will be so ga-ga over your staging that they overlook checking comparables. Remember, price sells, staging and photos just sell faster. *Smart Tip:* If your home is not right-priced, it still won't sell.

Chapter 5 Roundup

Smart Essentials PREPARE :: What You Have Learned

▶▶ Create "Stop the car, Honey!" curb appeal.

▶▶ Put your home in just-right condition.

▶▶ De-clutter, de-personalize, clean, clean, clean.

▶▶ Stage your home to sell faster with "Wow!" factor and photos.

▶▶ Avoid costly staging mistakes.

▶▶ Plan your photo shoot to beat the competition.

CHAPTER 6

SHOW

In this chapter you'll learn smart ways to:

1. **Reel in buyers by targeting your home's hottest features.**

2. **Offer incentives to stand apart.**

3. **Beat the competition with a better price.**

As we stressed in Chapter 4, your home's listing price is your most important marketing tool. There's no way around it: One tool does not do the entire job of marketing your home for a fast sale at a great price. Read on to learn how you can use other tools to reel in your buyer.

TARGET THE RIGHT FEATURES

You may think you're selling a home, but what you are really selling is a collection of features. After all, most buyers shop for homes with a "needs and wants" list. They will look at homes that match their needs — e.g., three bedrooms and two baths — but they'll buy the home that offers the most "wants" for the money.

To effectively market your home, first identify all its special features that would appeal to today's buyers, and especially your target buyers. Work together with your agent to do this. You know your home better than anyone; take the time to list everything about your home that might engage a buyer's "wants" list. (Save any problems you know about for the property disclosure statement.[††])

[††] ***Property Disclosure***
Sometimes called "seller disclosure" or "residential disclosure," property disclosure refers to the seller's responsibility to inform buyers about the "material facts" of a property, including information about its condition, legal status and other factors that could affect the home's value and desirability.

Property disclosure is especially important to buyers, who want to know as much as possible about a property before investing in it. Although you may be reluctant to divulge information you think might lower your home's value, failure to disclose known problems puts you at greater risk of being sued by buyers who discover those problems after the sale.

State requirements vary regarding how much and what kinds of information sellers are required to divulge about a home. Be sure to ask your real estate agent or attorney about property disclosure requirements in your state.

Below are some attractive features that could sway buyers to make an offer on your home rather than the competition's.

Hot Features

- ▶ Great view — water, mountains, landmark, cityscape
- ▶ Water feature — pond, lake, fountain, hot tub, pool (but a negative in some areas)
- ▶ Granite/stone countertops
- ▶ Stainless-steel appliances
- ▶ High-end master bathroom
- ▶ Hardwood and/or ceramic/stone floors
- ▶ Sunroom, screened porch
- ▶ Multi-car garage
- ▶ Fireplace(s)
- ▶ High ceilings/cathedral ceiling
- ▶ Generous storage
- ▶ Privacy
- ▶ Low-maintenance features
- ▶ Low property taxes

Location Perks

Point out how your home's location contributes to a convenient, safe and desirable lifestyle. "Walkability" — what's in walking distance of the home — is of growing interest to today's buyers. Emphasize your home's proximity to:

- ▶ Employment centers
- ▶ Public transportation

▶ Highways and major thoroughfares
▶ Good schools
▶ Places of worship
▶ Parks, playgrounds, recreational and fitness opportunities
▶ Shopping, restaurants and entertainment
▶ Cultural venues
▶ Community events and activities

Green Features

More than ever, buyers are paying attention to the operating costs of a home — that is, utility bills. You can attract their attention by pointing out your home's energy-saving features:

▶ Energy-efficient windows and doors
▶ High-efficiency water heater, A/C, furnace, boiler, etc.
▶ Extra insulation in walls and attic
▶ Geothermal or solar system, wind turbine
▶ Newer energy-efficient appliances — stove, refrigerator, dishwasher, washer/dryer, etc.
▶ Light-reflecting roofing shingles
▶ Low-flow faucets, toilets and showerheads
▶ Recycling, water catchment, compost
▶ Use of CFL or LED light bulbs throughout

If your home is energy efficient — especially more so than comparable homes — print out a year's worth of utility bills and make them available to buyers. Consider contracting for an energy audit to prove green efficiency. Many buyers will also be attracted to homes that have green building materials because they're made from renewable resources and minimize harmful fumes.

Upgrades And Improvements

Today's buyers are savvy about finding out what you originally paid for your home. One way to help justify your home's higher value today is to demonstrate how you've upgraded your home while owning it. Knowing that major items have been recently replaced or upgraded will give buyers confidence that *they* won't be saddled with those expenses anytime in the near future. Be sure to note date of replacement/improvement and warranty information, as applicable.

Here's a checklist to jog your memory:
- ▶ Roof
- ▶ Windows/doors
- ▶ Appliances
- ▶ Heating/air-conditioning system(s)
- ▶ Exterior siding/paint
- ▶ Electrical
- ▶ Lighting and fans
- ▶ Internet/TV cable/network or WiFi
- ▶ Plumbing
- ▶ Flooring/carpeting
- ▶ Cabinets/countertops/built-ins
- ▶ Room remodels
- ▶ Additions/space modifications
- ▶ Septic
- ▶ Landscaping/fencing
- ▶ Well

OFFER INCENTIVES

Incentives are extras you can offer buyers to put your home a cut above the competition. If your home is in the middle or bottom of the pack compared to what your competition is selling, adding incentives to your listing could boost your home's appeal. *Smart Tip:* Consult your agent and think carefully about whether to offer particular incentives as part of your listing—to attract more buyer attention—or to save them for negotiating leverage once a buyer makes a purchase offer.

Here are some incentives to consider:

💬 **Seller contribution**—paying a specified portion of buyer's loan points, settlement costs, first-year HOA or condo fees, etc., or offering a redecorating or repair allowance.

💬 **Conveyances**—leaving behind appliances, big-screen TV, pool table, perfect-fit furniture, kids' gym set, hot tub, patio furniture, riding lawn mower, fitness equipment or other items that wouldn't normally convey with the home—especially items you don't want to move anyway.

- **Immediate possession** — allowing buyers to move in immediately after settlement.

- **Loan assumption** — if your mortgage rate is attractive compared with current rates.

- **Home warranty** — for as little as $300, a one-year warranty covering all the home's major systems. Some programs even cover appliances.

- **Services** — availability of continuing services for lawn care, home security systems or house cleaning (by prearrangement). Consider a service you can do personally, e.g., cook a gourmet meal, create an etching or watercolor of the home, give frequent flyer miles, offer guitar lessons or do the buyer's taxes.

- **Seller financing** — offering to finance some or all of your home's purchase.

- **Lease/purchase** — if you don't need your funds immediately, let the buyer rent with a delayed settlement, provided you are sure the purchaser will eventually qualify for the loan. Part of the rental could apply toward the down payment.

Costly Incentive Mistakes To Avoid

Mistake #1: Paying more in incentives than needed. Incentives offer an ideal trifecta of uses: advertising them from the beginning, tossing them in during negotiations, or reigniting a listing that isn't selling. But use incentives wisely. Offering too much in the way of incentives can reduce your bottom-line walkaway cash.

Solution: Be sure to put the maximum amount you'll pay for incentives in writing. Avoid costly big-ticket giveaways, such as a sports car or cruise, or incentives buyers don't value. (Better to reduce your price instead.) Avoid mistaking the odd conveyance as a sweetener, when really you're just off-loading your junk.

Mistake #2: Increasing price to recoup incentives or making a deal-killing "cash back at settlement" offer. Today's competitive price market has put a kibosh on the "raise your price to cover costs" strategy. Without lender approval for incentives such as cash for repairs, tight appraisal guidelines don't allow room for buyers to overpay and get cash back from the seller.

Solution: Consider lowering your listing price instead of offering a fake incentive. It's better to offer a credit at settlement, perhaps for a "decorating allowance," or make repairs or upgrades yourself before listing.

Mistake #3: Going over the top with seller financing, lease to own or even renting property. Becoming a lender or a landlord can be a costly distraction.

Solution: Keep your eye on the prize: selling your home. Seller financing has its place (although rare) when the seller owns the property outright, doesn't need cash from the sale and prefers installment payments for income (and reduced taxes). One seller-financing scenario is to help a buyer with, say, a 10% down-payment loan (if the lender allows). The buyer with 10% in cash would then have a 20% down payment and be able to avoid private mortgage insurance. Remember, if the buyer defaults, you'll have the headache of a foreclosure and eviction on your hands. Plus, as the secondary creditor behind the primary lender, there may not be much left to pay you back.

A lease/purchase (also, rent-to-buy, lease option) has its place, especially in markets where many tenants are foreclosed homeowners with bad credit. A rent-to-buy scenario can open a larger buyer pool. Just know you'll forgo any appreciation upon final settlement because the sale price is agreed to upon initial signing. Buyer tenants may want to record the lease/purchase agreement with the county to ensure you don't sell the home to someone else instead. *Smart Tip:* Keep these incentives for just the right buyer.

SPREAD THE WORD

Once you've collected photos and all the information about your home — including contract terms you're willing to offer buyers — incorporate that information in the listing with your agent. Your agent will use the information and photos to construct your online listing with the local MLS, which eventually will feed into other online real estate sites. Make sure the information buyers see online about your home is complete, accurate and compelling.

How else can you spread the word about your home sale?

💬 **Dedicated web page** — make sure the page is searchable by your home's address and linked to the MLS site, if you're listed.

💬 **Social media** — regular updates on Facebook, Twitter, etc.

💬 **Print ads** — in local newspapers, magazines, home guides.

💬 **Yard signs** — posted on your property and at strategic locations in your neighborhood, with riders to property website or instant text with property details.

💬 **Brochure/fliers** — made available outside your home in a weather-proof container and inside your home for visiting buyers. Spring for high-quality paper and color printing to enhance photos.

💬 **Display** — set on an easel or in an album inside your home with photos and large-print text emphasizing features, area maps, upgrades, green features and contract incentives.

💬 **Personal contacts** — email or talk with friends, neighbors, relatives and coworkers; post fliers on bulletin boards and in newsletters of organizations you are affiliated with.

💬 **Broker open house** — arrange with your agent to introduce your home to office colleagues and other agents/brokers who can recommend it to their buyers.

Costly Open House Mistake To Avoid

Mistake: Thinking open houses are a relic of the past. Some sellers believe open houses only generate buyer leads for the agent rather than sell the house.

Solution: Yes, public open houses tend to attract more looky-loos and nosy neighbors than serious buyers. But they can draw a crowd. Also, be open to other types of opens. Office opens (also, caravan, tour) are private showings for the agents in your listing agent's office or company. Broker opens are similar for co-brokers in the area. It's smart to bring out both groups to preview your listing, perhaps on a weekday when the property is "coming soon" before it hits the MLS, because these agents/brokers are working with serious buyers. Consider an extreme by-invitation open, with catering, music, even builders and architects if the property has renovation potential or is a tear down. Another open variation targets an awesome feature, such as hot-air balloon rides from the helipad, yacht tours from your dock, horse rides around the stable, apple picking in a private orchard or driving golf balls from your backyard to the fairway. Let your agent be your guide.

MAKE SHOWINGS EASY

Be flexible about letting buyers and agents into your home. Buyers can have a very short attention span — especially when there's a large inventory of homes on the market to choose from.

If a buyer finds the time to visit your home with his or her agent, make sure they can get in! Your listing can indicate you would like a phone call before showings — say notice of 15 minutes to an hour in advance — so you can straighten up and/or leave the property before the buyer arrives. Be sure to turn off the dishwasher, washer, dryer, TV and radio. Don't leave unleashed pets (inside or out), important papers, mail, prescriptions, valuables, dirty litter boxes, pet bowls, rumpled beds or intense cooking smells.

Lockboxes are safe and easy. Allowing a lockbox on your door maximizes the ability of your agent and others to show your home while you're at work or out of town. Typically, agents will leave their business card inside your home, indicating that they visited while you were out. Your agent can then contact the showing agent to assess the home shopper's reaction to your property and find out whether an offer might be in the works. Feedback from these showings can help you tweak your home to better satisfy buyer preferences.

| Costly Showing Mistake To Avoid | **Mistake: Completely turning over selling to your listing agent and not being involved in the process.** Your agent may be good, but he or she still needs your cooperation and information to get your home sold. |

Solution: Be involved; you'll make more money. Don't go it alone . . . and don't leave your agent to go it alone. Set a listing date together ("coming soon"). Plan for the launch together. Solicit agent and buyer feedback together. Plan a price reduction schedule together. Work as a team. Be sure to avoid: limiting showing hours; making getting a key or access to your home difficult; or limiting access by locking the garage, storage, utility area or other rooms.

BE READY TO IMPROVE YOUR PRICE

No seller wants to hear the suggestion of a price reduction. After all, you researched and set your listing price to beat the competition. You put your home in tip-top, move-in-ready condition. You added some attractive incentives to your listing. And you gave your home the kind of exposure usually reserved for movie releases. So why should you drop your home's price? *Because it hasn't gotten an offer.*

Whenever you put a home on the market, one of five things will happen:

1. **Multiple offers:** A flurry of showings that produce multiple offers, resulting in sale price above asking. The property was underpriced, either by accident or design.

2. **Great offer:** Lots of showings produce one very strong offer, at or near asking price. The price was spot-on.

3. **Acceptable offer:** About 8 to 12 showings in 30 to 45 days produce an offer adequate to satisfy the seller and lead to settlement. This is the norm.

4. **No offers or unacceptable offers:** About 8 to 12 showings in 30 to 45 days but no offers or only ridiculous ones; a clear indication of a property problem. Agents and buyers are visiting the property, only to be disappointed on arrival. If the problem can be fixed (like bright paint colors), then fix it fast. If not, then the problem must be overcome with a better price.

5. **Nada:** Little or no showing activity. Agents and buyers are looking at listing details and electing not even to visit. Clearly, the price exceeds the market's expectations.

How long should you wait before you make a price reduction? That depends on your market and your timetable. If you really need to sell your home, two to four weeks of buyer inattention may be enough to warrant a price drop. If your home hasn't sold within the average days on market (DOM) of being listed, think price reduction. If comparable homes in your area have been selling quickly while yours became a wallflower, reduce your price. If more similar homes have come on the market below your price since you listed, you need a price improvement.

The market may have changed since you first listed your home. You may have over-estimated the value of your property. Other homes may have reduced their prices. Whatever. A price cut is the answer if you want to sell your home anytime soon.

Your agent can advise you how much of a price reduction you should consider. Perhaps 5% would do the trick; 10% would be more likely. Be aware, though, that a tiny price drop is not likely to spark the new-on-the-market attention your home sale needs. Having been on the market for a while, serious buyers have already passed on your property. To get them back in the game, you need to motivate them — and attract newcomers in the market — with a significant price reduction. Again, trust your agent's advice.

Costly Price Reduction Mistake To Avoid

Mistake: Dropping your price a teeny-weenie smidge. Small price drops simply don't get noticed.

Solution: Take off enough to re-launch demand in a whole different price bracket. Most buyers search online or on the MLS by looking in a price range. That's because a drop-down menu typically offers a set range of prices. Reduce your price to interest a fresh segment of buyers, for example, from $324,000 to $299,900. In lower ranges, price drops may be in $10,000 increments. In above-average price ranges, the increment may be $25,000. With luxury properties you may need a $100,000 reduction to get added bounce. The lower you go, the faster you will sell. In a falling price market, you'll want to go the extra reduction to stay "ahead of the market."

Smart Tip: Don't stop there. To get max attention, have your agent update the MLS listing with a "new price," do agent opens mid-week, update listing sheets and the property website, mail new-price "now available" postcards and add a sign rider with "Great New Price!" Also, be ready to sweeten the deal with more select incentives until a sales contract is signed.

Once you get a purchase offer from a buyer, you will be in the enviable position of negotiating for a final sales contract. That's when Chapter 7 alone will pay for this book many times over!

Chapter 6 Roundup

Smart Essentials SHOW :: What You Have Learned

▶▶ Reel in buyers by targeting your home's hottest features.

▶▶ Offer incentives to stand apart from the competition.

▶▶ Spread the word to the largest buyer pool.

▶▶ Make showings easy to schedule and provide access.

▶▶ Beat the competition with a better price.

▶▶ Avoid costly showing and price-reduction mistakes.

Smart Essentials

Page	Essential Note

NEGOTIATE

In this chapter, you will learn smart ways to:

1. Size up buyers to weed out low-ballers.

2. Evaluate every offer by the money.

3. Counteroffer like a riverboat gambler.

So what do you expect? Multiple, full-price, all-cash, no-contingency offers? They happen. But if they don't in your case, welcome to the high-wire art of negotiating. Is it the right offer? Should you take it? Is there a better offer out there? With this chapter you'll learn how to make real money and avoid the costliest deal-killing mistakes.

For starters, understand that everybody wants the same thing: You want to sell, your buyer wants to buy and your agent wants to close the deal. Relax. Every offer is an opportunity to get the best deal you can without losing the buyer.

Also, consider the market. You can negotiate more aggressively in a seller's market — not so much when buyers have the edge. If an offer comes in close to your hoped-for bottom line, then accept it and dance your way to settlement. Even if you are in a seller's market, be careful not to negotiate a price higher than the buyer's appraisal will support. Tread softly in negotiations if your home has been on the market a long time, it's had few recent showings or low interest from showings, you've had no other offers and see none on the horizon, you've moved (paying double mortgage, utilities, staging furniture, etc.) or recent comps show prices dropping. In a declining market, today's price will look great in six months.

ACE YOUR CONTRACT

When you receive a signed offer, you'll discuss the terms and buyer's qualifications with your agent. Either your listing agent, a seller's agent or a buyer's agent will have the information you need to determine whether the buyer is qualified to buy your home. (We'll talk more about sizing up buyers in a bit.)

Every seller has three basic options when presented with an offer. You can accept it as is, reject it outright, or make a written counteroffer — the sooner the better. You should continue to keep the home on the market. Until you sign a contract, buyers can withdraw an offer should they become stricken with "buyer's remorse." If you intend to counteroffer, do so immediately — buyers are in the mood to buy when they make an offer, but moods can change quickly.

Remember, whether full price or less, the first offers you get from buyers often turn out to be the best you'll see. Your first 30 days on the market are critical because a backlog of buyers often exists. These buyers have been looking and waiting for a home just like yours to come on the market. Even if your first offer isn't what you had hoped for, rejecting it outright means you don't have the opportunity to negotiate with buyers who have shown interest in purchasing your home. It could be a long wait before another serious buyer does the same.

◆ ◆ ◆

Essential Takeaway

Essential Takeaway: *Sometimes even a low offer can be turned into the bottom-line deal you are looking for — but you have to negotiate to get there!*

◆ ◆ ◆

Negotiating the sale price and terms sometimes means walking a tightrope between the highest price the buyer is willing to pay and the lowest price you can accept. Arriving at an agreement may take patience, psychology, flexibility — and intuition. Keep the dialogue going until you agree on price and terms. It's not unusual to exchange two or three counteroffers before a contract is reached.

The negotiation process is where top-notch real estate agents really earn their fees. First, they have training and experience in bringing sellers and buyers to terms acceptable to both. Second, they act as a buffer between sellers and buyers, helping to neutralize emotions and keep animosities at bay. Third, top agents know all the possible contract terms that can be brought into play to protect your interests while crafting a contract that meets the buyer's needs as well. Your agent is in a unique position to facilitate a win-win contract for both you and your buyer.

Your signed acceptance of a written offer becomes your sales contract. Except for removing any contingencies, this document is the binding basis for the sale. Contingencies are for your protection as well as the buyer's, because you don't want to be tied to a buyer who can't deliver.

◆ ◆ ◆

Essential Takeaway

Essential Takeaway: *Exercise confidence and patience as the buyer weighs your counteroffers. Be forthcoming with all the information requested and call attention to all the areas of agreement. Stay positive. When disagreements occur, iron out all the small issues before getting down to any real stumbling block later, when most items are already agreed upon.*

◆ ◆ ◆

ANATOMY OF A SALES CONTRACT

The sales contract is a very important document. The terms defined in writing will be used throughout the transaction and become the legal basis for the transfer of your property.

Depending on the situation, terms and conditions will vary. Most important is making sure you know who pays what and what the costs of those items are to sharpen your pencil on a net-proceeds evaluation. Here are some typical points contained in a contract:

● Property description, including separate personal property—conveyances—that will transfer to the buyer with the home.

● Earnest money[††], who holds it and what happens to it in case the buyer defaults on the contract.

> [††] ***Earnest Money***
> Also called the "deposit," earnest money is a partial down payment that the buyer submits by check with a purchase offer to show the buyer's good faith in buying the home. Normally, earnest-money deposits are returned to the buyer if contract contingencies are not met. In other cases, sellers may keep this money as compensation if the buyer defaults on the contract.

● Sale price of the home.

● Amount of the buyer's down payment (including earnest money). This amount, plus the mortgage loan, equals purchase price.

● Financing clause — the amount and type of mortgage the buyer intends to obtain.

● Discount points and who pays them.

● Contingencies that will determine the fulfillment of the contract. (More on contingencies below.)

● Date of settlement or closing.

● Possession date and any pre- or post-settlement occupancy agreement if the seller wishes to stay in the home after settlement and pay rent, or the buyer needs to occupy before settlement.

● Signatures of seller(s) and buyer(s).

Now let's dig deeper.

Conveyances

Some home sellers leave behind awnings, draperies, blinds, shades and rods bought to fit specific windows. Sometimes buyers ask for personal property such as garden tools, or if you are moving to an apartment or condo, you may offer to leave the tools. Decide which items could convey with the home that a buyer might want *and* that could save you money on moving costs.

◆ ◆ ◆

Essential Takeaway

Essential Takeaway: *Personal property items — and personal property that you would rather not take with you — can be useful "sweeteners" in your negotiations with a buyer. For example, your buyers want the kids' playset out back and they've also offered a price lower than what you listed for. Give them the playset (you really didn't want to move it anyway), and stick to your price. If your sale hinges on the conveyance of an item, be prepared to let it go to reach a contract.*

◆ ◆ ◆

Financing Contingency

The financing clause is a common contingency that states the contract will be void if the buyer cannot obtain a specified type of mortgage at a certain rate (or better) within a specified period of time. This time period must be realistically based on how long it is taking lenders in your area to process loans. *Smart Tip:* Buyers who are pre-approved for a mortgage are ideal because you can be reasonably certain of their financial ability to go to settlement — and getting there will take less time!

Depending on the loan type your buyer is applying for, a typical waiting period can be between 30 and 90 days, but sometimes more or less. Some lenders can even give same-day approval — with stipulations — using electronic mortgage underwriting, which relies on credit-scoring statistical models. The difference in waiting time largely depends on whether it is conventional[††] or government-backed FHA/VA[††] financing. (If you are providing the financing, it's up to you and your attorney.)

The biggest factor influencing how long it takes for loan approval is the borrower's preparation. Good credit and a complete application are the best ways for buyers to get a loan approved quickly.

[††] *Conventional Financing*

Conventional mortgages are those *not* guaranteed by government organizations such as the Federal Housing Administration (FHA) and the Department of Veterans Affairs (VA). Loans that meet standards set out by the federally chartered agencies Fannie Mae and Freddie Mac are considered "conforming" loans, while others — e.g., larger jumbo loans — are considered "non-conforming" loans.

Typically, conventional financing can be obtained more quickly than FHA/VA financing, depending on appraisal caseload, amount of time needed for credit check and income verification, and other lender requirements.

[††] *FHA/VA Financing*

Appraisals, credit check and verifications of employment and deposits are always done first for loans guaranteed by the FHA and VA. After the property meets specifications and all documents are received by the private lender, then the loan is usually sent to the FHA or VA for approval. Some lenders are approved for "direct endorsement" and "VA-automatic," where applications do not need to be sent to the FHA or VA. If approved, a survey and pest inspection are ordered. Total time may be up to 90 days in peak periods.

Both the FHA and VA mandate certain types of limitations not encountered with conventional loans. For example, the FHA prohibits sellers from contributing to buyers' down payments.

◆ ◆ ◆

Essential Takeaway

Essential Takeaway: *Show flexibility in evaluating a buyer's need for FHA or VA financing. These programs allow buyers to purchase with smaller down payments and somewhat lower credit scores—which may be just the ticket for a buyer to purchase your home.*

◆ ◆ ◆

Discount Points

As we discussed in Chapter 3, loan discount points are a one-time interest charge prepaid to the buyer's lender to lower the buyer's mortgage interest rate. These points can be paid by the buyer, or you—the seller—can offer to pay some or all points.

With today's higher down-payment requirements for mortgages, many otherwise qualified buyers find it difficult to amass enough cash to cover both the down payment and settlement costs for a home purchase. *Smart Tip:* By paying some or all of the buyers' points, you help them finance at a lower interest rate and lower the amount of cash they need to go to settlement. Also, the buyer can deduct those points as mortgage interest.

◆ ◆ ◆

Essential Takeaway

Essential Takeaway: *Offering to pay the buyer's discount points could clinch the deal for a buyer interested in your home. You might even be able to negotiate a higher sale price in the bargain! (Be sure, however, that an increased sale price will be supported by the appraisal.)*

◆ ◆ ◆

Other Contingencies

Contingencies (informally called "escape" or "kick-out" clauses) are contract conditions that must be met within a specified period of time for your home sale to go to settlement. If any condition goes unfulfilled, the party who benefits from the contingency is legally free to pull out of the deal.

Contingencies *buyers* may want to negotiate for, in addition to the financing clause:

🔊 **Appraisal:** An appraisal contingency allows the buyer to back out if the appraisal is less than the home's contracted sale price. This clause makes it essential that you do not negotiate an above-market sale price, say, to cover contributions you make to the buyer for discount points, redecorating allowance, etc.

🔊 **Inspections:** These contingencies hinge the sale on three types of professional inspections: home inspections (structural or mechanical), environmental inspections and pest inspections. More on these shortly, in counteroffers.

Some states and many title companies and mortgage lenders require certain inspections — with satisfactory results — before the home sale can go to settlement. (If an inspection is required by the state, the seller usually bears the expense.) The most common requirement is a "pest letter" or other similarly named document, certifying the property is free of damage from wood-destroying insects.

Two types of sales-contract inspection contingencies are possible. A "general contingency" (also, "take it or leave it") inspection clause stipulates that the contract is contingent on the buyer receiving a "satisfactory" professional home inspection. This contingency allows buyers to walk away from the contract without a penalty if they dislike *anything* in the inspection report.

A "specific contingency" spells out particular criteria that must be met before the buyer can back out of the contract — for example, the owner's failure to fix a problem identified by the inspection. The buyer cannot just walk away for any reason. *Smart Tip:* Specific rather than general inspection contingencies favor sellers. More in counteroffers ahead.

Home sale: Most often used in a buyer's market, a home-sale contingency (or contingent sale offer) makes the buyers' purchase offer contingent on the sale of their old home. *Smart Tip:* If you decide to accept such an offer, be sure to include a "release clause" that limits the amount of time the buyers have to sell their home. This allows you to continue to market your home and accept backup offers in case the first buyer does not sell the old home within the specified time frame.

Clear title: If title defects are found — say, a dispute about ownership — the buyer can withdraw from the contract. If there are any liens, from unpaid contractors, taxes or child support, you'll need to pay them off before settlement.

Condo or co-op board approval: This contingency is common where board approval is required for ownership.

Review of CC&R documents: CC&R is short for Covenants, Conditions and Restrictions. Buyers review these rules that govern associations such as condominiums, cooperatives, homeowners associations and sometimes even historic districts. CC&Rs also include an association's budget and reserves.

Attorney approval: Buyers may want to have an attorney review and approve the contract. Some states require attorney review.

Contingencies *you* may want to negotiate for:

Inspection: This is usually a modification to the buyer's inspection clause, setting a deadline for inspection, limiting how long the buyer has to notify you of problems found during inspection and setting a maximum amount you will pay for repairs.

🗨 **Home of choice:** This contingency — mostly used in seller's markets — would allow you time to find a replacement home before your sale goes to settlement.

🗨 **Court approval:** When a property is being sold to settle an estate, a court-approval contingency may be required.

🗨 **Attorney approval:** You too may want an attorney to review the contract to ensure that your interests are protected.

⸻ ◆ ◆ ◆ ⸻

Essential Takeaway

Essential Takeaway: You can use contingencies to smooth acceptance of the contract without delaying the buyer's decision to purchase your home. Keep in mind that just because a contingency would allow your buyer to back out of the contract, doesn't mean your buyer will do so. After all, your buyer is signing a contract because he or she really does want to purchase your home.

⸻ ◆ ◆ ◆ ⸻

Possession Date And Occupancy

Normally, buyers want to take possession and occupy the home immediately upon settlement. (That means you and your things must be out by settlement.) However, other arrangements are possible.

Perhaps you need an additional 10 days or two weeks beyond settlement before you can move into your next home. You could negotiate with your buyer to remain in the home, delaying occupancy for that period of time. The contract should spell out how long you are allowed to live in the home after settlement and how much money you will pay the buyer for that privilege. Often, the rental amount is a prorated portion of the buyer's mortgage payment.

Another possibility: Your buyers may ask for an "early occupancy" agreement — paying a prorated portion of your mortgage payment — if they have to vacate their current residence prior to settlement. Try to arrange temporary accommodations rather than occupancy; if the deal goes south, getting buyers out can be a hassle.

◆ ◆ ◆

Essential Takeaway

Essential Takeaway: *Assign a dollar value for any item or concession you give to the buyer during negotiations — keeping an eye on the bottom line. This will be easier for physical items — such as personal property — than for concessions such as a home-sale contingency. Remember, though, concessions have real value to buyers; use them to get the price you want and a signed contract!*

◆ ◆ ◆

Now down to brass tacks.

How To Size Up Buyers

You are looking for a serious buyer who can get to settlement on your contract — otherwise you're just wasting your valuable time and resources. Here's how to determine whether you are dealing with a serious buyer:

🗩 **Deposit:** One way to find out is to require a significant deposit. Ask about local custom; sometimes the figure will be up to 5% of the sale price. Just be sure the deposit is large enough — painful to walk away from — to overcome potential buyer's remorse.

🗩 **Loan application.** What is the status of the buyers' loan application, or haven't they even begun? Ask for their application (Form 1003), credit scores, pre-approval or rate-lock expiration dates, if any. At minimum, get a description of the buyer's finances.

🗩 **Qualifications.** If it's an all-cash or high-down-payment offer, get proof of the source of funds. If the buyer is self-employed, get info on the business and how long it has been in operation. A two-income couple make a stronger buyer than a single buyer with dinged credit. Debt-to-income (DTI) ratios[††] are a good guide. If the buyer is credit-challenged or has a small down payment, you may want to offer some financial help — or not.

†† *Debt-To-Income (DTI) Ratios*

DTIs are useful to lenders. They express how much of the borrower's income would go toward paying a mortgage and other debt obligations. For example, a lender might set a maximum DTI of 28/36. The first number is the front-end DTI: the monthly mortgage payment (principal, interest, taxes, insurance; PITI) divided by income. In our example, the lender would want that number to be no higher than 28. The second number is the back-end DTI: PITI plus all recurring debts divided by income. In the example, the maximum would be 36. Lenders like lower DTIs.

● **Pre-approval.** If the buyer has lender pre-approval, dig deeper to confirm that pay stubs, bank statements, tax returns and W-2s were provided. Compare the offer price and pre-approval letter or buyer qualifications to determine whether you might be getting a low-ball bid because the buyer truly can't afford to pay more. Be sure the lender is a reputable lender and that the buyer hasn't simply been "pre-qualified" based on the buyer's credit score and oral statements. A pre-approval letter tells you how much the buyer can afford. Check dates and whether the lender commitment is coming to an end — creditworthiness can change.

● **Type of financing.** Give thumbs up to a buyer applying for a conventional 30-year conforming loan. If the buyer is going to the FHA or VA, you may be expected to negotiate paying the buyer's points. If the buyer is trying for an option or interest-only loan, or has a bankruptcy, foreclosure or dinged credit, the risk is higher that the buyer won't get approved and your sale could fall through. *Smart Tip:* Set a "drop dead date" to receive the buyer's loan-commitment letter.

● **Down payment.** Find out how much the buyer will put down and get proof of funds. The larger the down payment, the better the interest rate the buyer will qualify for (increasing buying power) and the less likely lenders will reject the buyer. Is gift money involved? Make sure the gift money has been received — and documented as a gift, not a loan — as soon as possible rather than right before settlement.

● **Sale of buyer's home.** First-time buyers with nothing to sell, buyers with a sales contract on their current home, or buyers who have already sold their home are ideal. *Smart Tip:* If a buyer must sell his or her home first, check the MLS for days on market, location, price reductions and details and get an opinion from your agent about whether the property will sell in time to settle on your sale to the buyer. If the buyer's sale is pending, get a copy of the sales contract and info on the buyer's buyer, if possible. After all, if the buyer's sale is iffy, then your sale could be iffy, too.

● **Nickel and dime.** A clean contract has few to no contingencies. If a buyer presents a blizzard of small demands, from conveying personal property to trivial repairs, from wanting you to pay for every inspection to a far-off settlement date, you may be working with a nickel-and-dimer — not an ideal buyer.

● **Representation.** Talk with your listing agent about the reputation of the buyer's agent and brokerage. The quality of the offer presentation can be a clue, especially if language is sloppy or provisions are boilerplate. Poor buyer's agents can be a headache in the settlement process. Prefer a buyer with strong representation.

● **Other.** Revealing clues to motivation and intention may include: how many homes the buyer has previewed; how long the buyer has been looking with an agent; whether the buyer has made any offers recently on other homes; whether the buyer has sold a current home and needs a new one fast. Serious buyers may volunteer this information in a cover letter.

COUNTEROFFER LIKE A RIVERBOAT GAMBLER

Smart Ways To Counter On Price

● **Smart price counter #1:** Stay firm on your price but sweeten the deal with items that buyers value. This is where you trade the incentive cards you held back from the listing, rather than lowering the price. Be selective, considering:

▶ **Appliances** — you'll save on moving expenses, too.

▶ **Allowances** for repairs or decorating.

▶ **Move-in condition** — buyers may pay more than your cost to accomplish it.

▶ **Home warranty** — gives buyers peace of mind for the first year.

▶ **Longer contingency periods** — helps buyers find financing, sell their home, etc.

▶ **Pay some settlement costs**—points, buy down the interest rate, etc.

Put simply, give buyers something to make them think they "got a deal."

🗩 **Smart price counter #2:** Buyers present a low initial offer to find out your *real* price, and assume you'll settle halfway in between their offer and your list price. Consider a partial price counter at 30% of the price difference, not 50%, and bring the buyer up beyond the "meet in middle" expectation. Example: Buyer offered $10,000 below list price. Buyer expects to settle at $5,000 below list (50% of difference). Instead, lower your price $3,000 (30% of difference), and throw in sweeteners from Counter #1.

🗩 **Smart price counter #3:** Accept a lower price offer, but ask for faster settlement (saves you carrying costs) or ask the buyer to pay for any inspections. Consider specifying a maximum amount for repairs—an amount or percentage of the sale price—as a trade for accepting the buyer's lower price.

Smart Ways To Counter On Contingencies

You'll want to shape contingencies to your favor, and use other contingencies as a counterbalance to any concessions you make, like price. Although contingencies smooth the acceptance of a contract, they also provide escape hatches for buyers (or sellers) who change their minds and want to bail. Here are some smart strategies.

🗩 **Financing counter:** Require a mortgage pre-approval letter. *Smart Tip:* Check the contingency for maximum interest rate, which should be half to 1% higher than current rates. If it's too low, counter with a higher rate. If you've had a lender approve your condominium or co-op property, require that the buyer apply with that lender.

🗩 **Sale & settlement counter** (also, "home sale" or "wipe-out" clause): Counter to keep your home on the market while the buyer tries to sell his or hers. In the event that you get another offer, the first buyer has a period of time to secure financing (such as a bridge loan) or remove the S&S contingency. If they don't, release the agreement (and return the deposit) so you can negotiate with the new buyer. Remember, buyers may not want to visit your property if it's under an S&S contingency ("contract pending"), fearing they won't get the home. If you have other offers or expect them, consider rejecting this contingency and encourage the first buyer to sell quickly. Just be aware that when — or *if* — the buyer comes back to your unsold home, the offer may be lower.

● **Home inspection counter:** Avoid a "take it or leave it" clause that lets the buyer cancel the contract after an unsatisfactory home inspection of mechanical systems and structure. Counter with a confirmation of your right to make repairs or credit the cost above the "as is" repairs threshold. Put a cap on the repairs amount you'll pay. This counter keeps the contract alive in the event that inspections find problems. Some options: (1) You can offer to escrow an amount to pay future repairs. Contractor bids for big-ticket repairs may be needed to set that figure. (2) You can lower the sale price. (3) You can make repairs and pay for them yourself, especially if they are cosmetic ones, and the buyer doesn't want the bother. (4) Avoid having the buyer make repairs that you pay for while you're still in the house; it can delay your move if repairs take longer than expected. (5) Ask for a clause by which the buyer agrees not to require minor fix-ups of less than, say, $100 or $250.

● **Other inspections counter:** Inspection techniques and costs vary for environmental inspections (toxic mold, well, spring, septic, radon, underground oil, lead, asbestos, etc.) or pest inspections (termites, wood-destroying insects, ants, bees, rodents, etc.). Consider countering to have the buyer pay for inspections, not you. If you pay, specify the most you'll pay. Repair or replacement costs ("remediation") vary even more. Talk with your agent and consider doing inspections and repairs *before* listing, especially if your locality requires a "code inspection" by the seller. The more you deal with headaches early, the fewer headaches you'll face later. Some contingencies would require a zoning variance — say, to allow an in-home business, kennels or animals, parking an RV, school bus or truck cab, or installing a fence or pool. If approval is lengthy or unlikely, reject the contingency. If the property doesn't fit the buyer's needs as is, it's up to the buyer to improve it later.

| **Costly Appraisal Mistake To Avoid** | **Mistake: What if the appraisal comes in below the sale price?** An appraisal contingency allows the buyer to drop out if the appraisal comes in below the sale price. |

Even without an appraisal contingency, if the lender won't approve a loan for an over-value sale price, the financing contingency can kill the deal.

Solution: If the buyer fails to include an appraisal clause that gives the buyer the right to drop out if "property does not appraise," then the buyer must either make up the difference between the appraisal and sale price — effectively increasing the down payment — or forfeit the deposit and walk away from the deal. Although the buyer can dispute the appraisal or apply with another lender, these scenarios rarely produce a different outcome. You and the buyer are now caught between a rock and a hard place. If you don't reduce the price — or the buyer doesn't increase the down payment — the deal is dead. Meeting somewhere in the middle may be the best solution.

SETTLE YOUR SALE

Once you have a signed sales contract — hooray! During the time from contract to settlement, your agent will be shepherding the deal along, helping you fulfill your contract obligations.

You will need to make arrangements to let in inspectors and the appraiser. You'll start packing — if you haven't already moved out. You'll have to order and supervise any repairs required by the contract and send proof they've been accomplished — receipts and/or photos — to your buyer. And you'll need either to clean the place or hire a team to do it for you.

The last thing you want to do is flunk the walk-through inspection! This is when the buyer will take a final look at the home — just before settlement — to ensure any required repairs have been made and that the property is in the condition agreed upon in the contract. Be sure you've planned enough time after move-out for housecleaning or minor touch-ups to ensure the buyer doesn't balk — and delay settlement — over some minor detail that still needs attention.

Although settlement scenarios vary from area to area, three basic steps are always taken. You, as the seller, prove you have marketable title; the buyer pays for the property; and you give the buyer a deed or bill of sale. Settlement usually takes place in less than an hour or two.

CONGRATULATIONS!

Now that your home is sold, settled and your check's in your pocket, you can exhale, laugh and celebrate. Congratulations! When you sell your next home, you'll be even smarter!

If you know someone who is planning to sell soon, pay it forward by recommending SMART ESSENTIALS FOR SELLING YOUR HOME.

Again, high five, Smartie!

Chapter 7 Roundup

Smart Essentials NEGOTIATE :: What You Have Learned

▶▶ How to ace your contract.
▶▶ How to understand the anatomy of sales contracts.
▶▶ Smart facts from conveyances to contingencies.
▶▶ How to size up buyers to weed out low-ballers.
▶▶ How to evaluate every offer by the money.
▶▶ How to counteroffer price like a riverboat gambler.
▶▶ Smart counteroffers for contingency terms.
▶▶ What to do if property appraisal is low.

About The Series

SMART ESSENTIALS was written for you.

We know because you tell us. Our readers are smart, busy, capable people stressed by the fact that they only get one chance to get it right buying or selling real estate. You tell us on our *http://www.SmartEssentials.com* website and in your emails. You appreciate smart, useful, distilled information that goes straight to the point.

Certainly, our readers *can* swim through the tides of endless online articles searching for useful information. Certainly, our readers *can* slog through full length how-to books trying to glean the chapter here or there that they really need hidden in the general filler. But you're too smart for that. You appreciate concise ideas that can make you tens of thousands in profit when you sell real estate and save you thousands at the settlement table when you buy — or avoid costly mistakes you didn't have to make.

You want the information now. You want it smartly presented. You want it current for today's market. Mostly you want your information concise, concentrated and applicable to your situation.

🗩 Like the crazed bride who thanked us for advising that soon-to-be-newlyweds start looking for a home three months *after* the wedding.

🗩 Like the Canadian investor who appreciated learning that California charges a transfer tax on non-resident sales, so he bought in Nevada.

🗩 Like the thankful divorced Dad who bought two extra bedrooms for sleepovers on custody weekends.

🗩 And like the thankful parents who saved thousands over seven years (two serial college kids) by investing in rentable student housing because at their state university most students had to rent off-campus housing.

We also know most of our readers typically buy multiple SMART ESSENTIALS. Not only because most sellers are buyers and most buyers become sellers, but mostly because you have smart friends. You talk. Naturally. After all, you just spent the last few months consumed by one of the largest life-shaping transactions of your life. Who wouldn't need to vent?

That's why we wrote every SMART ESSENTIALS for you.

Let us know what you think. More important, when you run across one of those incredible little nuggets of street-smart wisdom during your transaction, email us or share it as a Smarties' Story on our website. We love your stories. And the thousands of other Smarties facing the same situation will thank you, too. Giving is sharing. And sharing is the best way we know to enhance love.

Looking forward to hearing from you!

Dan Gooder Richard
Series Editor

Dan Gooder Richard can be contacted at:

SMART ESSENTIALS
c/o Inkspiration Media
2724 Dorr Avenue, Suite 103
Fairfax, VA 22031
(703) 698-7750
SellingYourHome@SmartEssentials.com
http://www.SmartEssentials.com

About The Team

A venture the size of SMART ESSENTIALS requires an outstanding team. Dan Gooder Richard is the editor of the SMART ESSENTIALS series. Dan's first book, REAL ESTATE RAINMAKER®: Successful Strategies for Real Estate Marketing, was published by John Wiley & Sons in 2000. Dan's second book, REAL ESTATE RAINMAKER®: Guide to Online Marketing, was published by John Wiley & Sons in 2004. He is also creator of the RAINMAKER LEAD SYSTEM® now in use by thousands of real estate professionals nationwide. He and his wife, Synnove Granholm, founded GOODER GROUP® in 1983 and continue to manage the Fairfax, Virginia-based publisher of marketing materials for real estate and mortgage professionals. Hats off to Deborah Rhoney, our managing editor, principal writer and author of this SELLING guide. She puts the smart into the essentials. Amy Hausman, our marketing diva and writer, keeps the buzz going with every new publication. Special thanks to our web master, Tammy Waitsman, and our social media guru, Jesse Hickman, for making the online side of SMART ESSENTIALS truly click. Jane Rooney, our controller at Inkspiration Media, keeps us on track and on forecast. Stephanie Simmons keeps the service to readers stellar and makes the smallest detail her mission. A special thanks to David Wu of DW Design, whose branding and graphic design makes us all look good. To the entire team at SMART ESSENTIALS — thank you — we couldn't do it without you!

SMARTIES' CREED

🗨 **Express your voice** at *http://www.SmartEssentials.com* and you will be part of one of the world's smartest communities.

🗨 **Help others** get smarter for less. Simply share with two. And they tell two. Pay it forward 33 times and you can reach every person on Earth.

🗨 **Keep up to date** with one click, one post, one random act of selflessness and you'll help everyone to be smarter, happier, richer.

🗨 **Imagine** if everyone reading your voice did something today to improve others. The world would be a smarter place . . . and it all would be thanks to your original, selfless act to help others.

SMART TALK

The fact that you are reading this sentence tells us a lot about you. Clearly, you have a hunger for wisdom to increase your home-selling smarts. Having gotten this far, it's likely you've got insights, experiences and questions of your own to share. Now it's time to reach out to other Smarties by sharing your answers and questions at the Smart Talk knowledge center: http://www.SmartEssentials.com. *We'll all be smarter for it!*

Pay it forward at *http://www.SmartEssentials.com* today!

More Titles In The Best-Selling SMART ESSENTIALS Series

🗨 SMART ESSENTIALS FOR SELLING YOUR HOME
How To Get The Highest Price In The Shortest Time

🗨 SMART ESSENTIALS FOR BUYING A HOME
How To Get The Best Price And The Lowest Payment

🗨 SMART ESSENTIALS FOR REAL ESTATE INVESTING
How To Build Wealth In Rental Property Today

🗨 SMART ESSENTIALS FOR BUYING FORECLOSURES
Finding Hidden Bargains For Home Or Profit

🗨 SMART ESSENTIALS FOR COLLEGE RENTALS
Parent and Investor Guide To Buying College-Town Real Estate